A FIELD GUIDE TO
ARCHEOLOGICAL
SITES OF TEXAS

A FIELD GUIDE TO
ARCHEOLOGICAL SITES OF TEXAS

BY PARKER NUNLEY

★
TexasMonthlyPress

Texas Monthly Press
P.O. Box 1569
Austin, Texas 78767

Library of Congress Cataloging-in-Publication Data

Nunley, Parker
  A field guide to archeological sites in Texas / by Parker Nunley.
    p. cm.
  ISBN 0-87719-155-7 : $21.95. — ISBN 0-87719-154-9 (pbk.)
. $11.95
    1. Excavations (archaeology)—Texas. 2. Texas—Antiquities.
3. Indian of North America—Texas—Antiquities.
4. Archaeology—Texas—Field work. I. Title.
F388.N86 1989
976.4'01—dc20   89-20182
                                                      CIP

Table of Contents

Acknowledgments

Through the several years of one's professional life, there inevitably pass many people to whom one is indebted, and so I am indebted to many with whom I have been associated. Of those many, the following come to mind as particularly significant to me as an archeologist.

At the University of Texas, Austin, where I first began the study of anthropology with a specialty in archeology, I was especially influenced by the guidance of Drs. T. N. Campbell, E. Mott Davis, and Dee Ann Story (née Suhm). It was with them I began the formal study of archeology.

Also at the University of Texas, I had the pleasure of my first fieldwork experience digging with Herb Alexander at the Kyle Site. Later that same year I became a fieldworker with the Texas Archeological Salvage Project (TASP) under the direction of Ed Jelks. While with TASP I worked at digs under the supervision of LeRoy Johnson, Jr., Dee Ann Suhm, and Curtis Tunnell. Later, in 1962, I became responsible for fieldwork on my own and carried out the initial surveys at Columbus Bend and Livingston reservoirs and the excavations at Coon Tail Spin and other sites in the Amistad area under the general supervision of Lathal Duffield and Ed Jelks. Others at TASP with whom I exchanged ideas and information included Bill Davis, Dan Scurlock, Jim Corbin, Harry Shafer, Mark Parsons, John Greer, and Vaughn Bryant. I am deeply indebted to all of them.

Subsequently I worked in South Texas with Tom Hester and in the Caddoan area of Louisiana with Pete Gregory. The following year, I began studies in the then newly established graduate program of the Department of Anthropology at Southern Methodist University. There I was especially influenced by Drs. Joel Shiner, Fred Wendorf and Tony Marks, all of whom introduced new aspects of archeological analysis and description to me. It was also at SMU that I grew to know and to love R. King Harris that grand old man of Texas archeology. To all those friends and colleagues, I am especially grateful.

I also appreciate and acknowledge the cooperation and assistance of the following individuals and institutions for supplying information and illustrations: Dr. H. F. Gregory, director, Williamson Museum, Northwestern State University, Natchitoches, Louisiana; Dr. Tom Hester, director, Texas Archeological Research Laboratory, University of Texas, Austin; Billy R. Harrison, curator of anthropology, Panhandle-Plains Museum, West Texas State University, Canyon; Dave Ing, archeologist, Texas Parks and Wildlife Department, Austin; Jack Eaton, acting director, Center for Archeological Research, University of Texas, San Antonio; Helen Simons, archeologist, Texas Historical Commission, Austin.

Finally, I would like to acknowledge the support of my special friend and colleague, Dr. M. Christopher Nunley, who has read and commented on much of the work represented in this book and has contributed to this work in countless other ways. To her I am especially indebted.

To all these and others unmentioned I say, thanks, it's been fun.

Preface

Several years ago I decided to revisit a number of archeological sites in Texas that have in the last few years become part of the extensive system of parks, monuments, museums, and other public access areas that grace our state. I had originally visited many of the sites years earlier and knew that Texas had made great strides in acquisition, protection, and development of these resources, so I was curious to see how they had been incorporated into the public domain.

When I stopped by a local office of the Texas Tourist Bureau to get whatever information was available on the parks so I could plan my trip, I was surprised to learn that the Texas Department of Highways and Public Transportation, the parent agency of the Travel and Information Division, offered little information on archeology. Although the personnel I encountered were cheerful, efficient, and helpful concerning typical tourist information such as lodging, routes for possible itineraries, places to eat, amusements, and other commercial ventures and even provided me with maps and an excellent general guide to Texas towns and cities, there was almost no information available concerning archeology.

Subsequent contacts with the Texas Parks and Wildlife Department, the agency responsible for many of the sites I was interested in visiting, revealed a similar lack of information. Although brochures indicated facilities available, fees, hours of operation, types of use intended for each park, and other bits of general information, there was no single source for information concerning archeology. Furthermore, information about specific sites, even those designated as historic, was general and of little use in planning a trip that focused on Texas archeology.

Over several months, during which I contacted personnel at each of the several parks, wrote to various state agencies, consulted libraries and purchased Texas travel and guide books, I found no specific source concerning the archeological sites I was interested in visiting. I discovered that the best way one could find out about these sites was to visit them.

At the historic parks, I was struck by the absence (although many of them provided a standard interpretation of local archeological materials) of any general explanation of the significance of the particular site. Instead, the interpretation was set in the context of some abstract concept such as "stages" of sociocultural evolution. That type of presentation is valid and useful, but it assumes certain shared interests and competencies between the interpreter and the visitor. I am not sure such assumptions are justified. Too often I noticed visitors either wandering about in glazed-eyed information overload or vainly searching the displays and asking for more printed information. The genesis of this book was their need for a sourcebook of the archeology of Texas that contains both general and specific information and that will be of interest to veterans of Texas archeology as well as casual visitors. Insofar as it meets those ends, this book will have satisfied both its primary purpose, to convey useful information in accessible form, and its secondary purpose, to provide an example of the practice of critical anthropology.

1
Introduction

Archeology as seen by professionals often becomes so ingrained, so apparent, that they sometimes forget what interested them in the discipline in the first place. They tend to become involved in esoteric problems, discussed in highly stylized ways, and so lose the ability to communicate to those outside the profession. When they try to communicate with a wider audience, they tend to oversimplify to the point of redundancy. And so it has been in Texas.

Practically the only archeological interpretation at our state historic parks, for example, is some variation of the traditional presentation of the Paleo-American, Archaic, Late Prehistoric, and Historic stages. They are presented as a series of "just-so" stories that are about as satisfying to an even mildly inquiring mind as the tale of how the tiger got its stripes. The assumption is that this level of interpretation will be sufficient for the average visitor, and perhaps it is.

If, however, the visitor is not average, is either not particularly interested in archeology for its own sake or not particularly interested in standardized interpretation, then our parks have little to offer. One must be average to benefit the most from our public facilities. Of course, few of us fit comfortably into an average. After twenty years of teaching introductory archeology, I have learned that relatively few students enroll for average reasons. Instead, students tend to take such introductory courses because they believe them to be an interesting way to satisfy an elective requirement or, much less frequently, they are interested in archeological method and theory and want to pursue that interest more deeply. Similarly, I have found that most visitors to archeological sites fall into one of two types: those who are taking a break between activities such as swimming, eating, driving, or some other purposive activity and find that walking through the exhibits passes the time in a relatively pleasant way, and those who are genuinely interested in archeology and came to the park in pursuit of that interest. Neither type is average, and I believe that interpretive materials directed toward the average presuppose too much previous knowledge in the case of the casual visitor but do not supply enough information for those more involved in the subject.

A purpose of this book, then, is to supply information for the typical, not average, visitor to our publicly accessible archeological sites. Toward that end, the reader will find specific information about archeological sites in the various regions of Texas as well as general concepts of anthropology and archeology.

Of the thousands of known archeological sites in Texas, specific examples were selected for this book on the basis of four criteria: relevance, accessibility, security, and geographic distribution. The criteria together serve to identify those sites that will yield the broadest view of Texas archeology and yet not violate the ethics and confidences necessary to the practice of field archeology.

Relevance. It has been argued that any archeological site is important, and in a sense, this is true. It is true, but not practical. The fact is, some sites are more important than others. Relevance has long been one measure of the degree of importance of a site. By "relevance" is meant the amount of value a particular site is believed to have with regard to a certain kind of problem.

For example, establishing a sequence through time, a chronology, is a basic problem in archeology, and a site that appears to offer promise of data to solve this problem would have greater relevance in this regard than other, less promising sites. In light of this criterion, then, the Lubbock Lake Site is vastly more relevant than hundreds of other sites with similar artifact types, because it is a rare example of a well-stratified site that offers a unique opportunity to arrange artifacts in sequence through time.

So, although all sites are relevant in some way, most of the sites included in this book are highly relevant in one or more ways. The relevance of each is discussed in the site descriptions, since it was in most cases one of the primary reasons for preserving the site and making it publicly accessible.

Accessibility. At first it may seem strange that ease of access should have been a major consideration in selection of sites for inclusion here. After all, why should this be a factor in pursuit of important information? Actually, access to data is always a factor in any field of endeavor and should not be surprising here.

These sites may be safely and conveniently reached by the casual visitor. Although many sites in Texas meet the other criteria, they are not included if they are not relatively easy to visit—some require special permission to visit, and others are dangerous or require strenuous effort to reach.

Security. This criterion is important to protect our archeological heritage. For obvious reasons, archeological sites are correctly viewed as nonrenewable resources. Each site offers a unique record of past events, and once that record is destroyed, it cannot again be recreated. Every time a site is changed, either by human intervention or by natural forces, the record is altered; evidence of the past is destroyed. Yet, to study these sites, parts of them must be destroyed. A task of any conscientious visitor is to study a site in such a way as to increase the amount of collected and recorded information while holding destruction to a minimum.

Even casual visitors can cause severe damage. Activities such as picnicking or off-the-road driving, although not intended to be destructive, can destroy evidence. Deliberate destruction of sites is, unfortunately, all too common. All sites listed here are on public or private property where an attempt has been made to balance security concerns with those of accessibility. In most cases the sites are protected by law and are open only while park personnel are present. In the final analysis, however, it is up to each visitor to take the responsibility to ensure prudent security of these sites.

Geographic distribution. I have tried to choose appropriate sites in all regions of the state. One reason for this effort was to ensure that visitors would be able to locate a site reasonably near whatever place in Texas they might happen to be. Another, perhaps more important reason was to give an accurate impression of the scope of Texas archeology and the interrelationship between culture and geography.

Texas is a huge state with many strikingly different environments. To facilitate description and to illustrate a basic concept in archeology, this book divides the state into six major geographic regions: Panhandle-Plains, Central Prairies, Pineywoods, South Texas, Edwards Plateau/ Hill Country, and the Trans-Pecos. Sites have been selected within each of these regions in part because they satisfy the criteria outlined above and in part to illustrate the geographic and cultural diversity of the state.

The Present State of Texas Archeology

Although archeology in Texas has grown substantially in the last three decades, most of that growth has resulted in an avalanche of data that have yet to be systematically organized. That explosive, unsystematic development has led to a tremendous increase in artifact collections, professional archeologists, and bureaucratic regulation without a corresponding increase in theory and interpretation.

The last period of rapid, theoretically vapid growth was before World War II, when the Works Progress Administration (WPA) used archeology to create jobs that would not conflict with those of already employed workers. During the WPA days many sites were dug, artifacts were cleaned and cataloged, and formal, descriptive reports were filed—and forgotten. We face a similar situation in Texas today. Following a different rationale, the federal government, through direct and indirect funding of various aspects of the environmental protection acts, has been the major source of support for archeological work in Texas. Most of the money, now as during the WPA, has been provided for "conservation" archeology, formerly called "salvage" archeology.

One result has been the proliferation of groups organized to get and spend this money. Accompanying the organizational proliferation has been a corresponding rise in the number of government agencies charged with administering funds. Consequently, the intent of archeology has been reified from its traditional role in the United States as an effective adjunct of anthropology to a ghost of its WPA past, with corresponding emphasis on form and procedure rather than theory and meaning.

As an example of the growth in Texas archeology, consider the following. The number of archeologists has risen from perhaps twenty active professionals in the late fifties to well over one hundred today. Thirty years ago most of the archeological work in the state was concentrated at three centers—the University of Texas at Austin, Texas Tech University, and West Texas State University. Today approximately twenty public agencies are involved in archeology, and about that many more private organizations are involved directly in archeological work.

Although accessibility to this burgeoning archeological data base has increased some, the work has been overwhelmingly directed toward excavation, description, and formula reporting. Relatively little effort has been made to carefully formulate theory-based research or to interpret data. Public access has been severely limited in some ways.

Problems of public access have been recognized by professional archeologists in Texas, but it has been difficult to address them. One approach is marked by the increase in popular publications about Texas archeology. The present book is intended to add a new dimension to the recent efforts of professionals (Hester 1980; Turner and Hester 1985; Shafer 1986) to bring more Texas archeology to more people.

A book such as this would not have been possible thirty years ago. There were almost no archeological sites in Texas that met all four of the criteria for inclusion. In particular, there were no sites that were readily accessible and well secured. Today there are many well-secured sites easily accessible to public visitors. That happy difference has developed within the last twenty years under the guidance of the Texas Historical Commission with the cooperation and support of the people of Texas through their elected and appointed officials. Those important sites throughout the state will preserve and protect our archeological resources well into the future. Other sites need to be acquired, and still others require constant development of facilities. With proper citizen concern, this part of our common heritage will continue to grow and constitute an ever-increasing portion of our collective gift to the future.

Each archeological site offers something that can be understood only by physically visiting the site. Archeological sites must be visited to be understood, and it is toward that end that this book is directed.

References

Hester, Thomas R. 1980. *Digging Into South Texas Prehistory.* San Antonio: Corona.

Shafer, Harry J. 1986. *Ancient Texans: Rock Art and Lifeways Along the Lower Pecos.* San Antonio: Witte Museum.

Turner, Ellen Sue, and Thomas R. Hester. 1985. *A Field Guide to Stone Artifacts of Texas Indians.* Austin: Texas Monthly Press.

2
Archeology

It's been said that archeology is the study of the past, and archeologists have been compared to detectives who, after carefully sifting through the evidence, carefully reconstruct the past. Certainly, part of their work resembles that metaphor, and those reconstructions are what is most often displayed in museums and parks and printed in popular books. Archeology thus portrayed seems distant from the daily existence of most people who view the displays.

For some time I have felt that archeology loses much of its emotional impact by maintaining that distance between the people who view the exhibits and those, the archeologists, who create them. The problem is more pronounced in a country such as the United States, with relatively little historic depth, than it is in countries such as Mexico and Israel, where there is a great sense of historic continuity.

It is important to recapture that emotional moment, that intensity of feeling, when one realizes a kind of identity between the present and the past. I am referring to that feeling we have when we pick up an arrowhead and wonder at its maker, when we admire a bead or a necklace and imagine who must have last worn this frail remainder of our common humanity, or, in the more explicit sense of this book, when we visit these sites and experience a connection, an identity, between ourselves and those who have gone before.

The purpose of this section is to portray archeology in such a way as to help the casual visitor understand in a personal, emotional way the reconstructions developed from archeological work at the sites described in this book. My intent is to draw the reader into the network of customs and rituals that constitute modern archeology and thereby help form an identity with the process of reconstructing the past. The point of view described here allows us to form a bond of meaning, of relevance, between the facts of modern existence and those of the past. In this sense archeology, or anthropology in general, allows us a new point of reference. I call this existential archeology.

According to this view the purpose of archeology is to provide a satisfactory account of the past. There are a number of competing archeologies, each claiming to offer *the* authentic account and each having its followers. For example, religious archeologists give an account of giant human footprints associated with dinosaur tracks in the bedrock of the Paluxy River channel near Glen Rose, Texas, and their account has its followers. Counterpoised to it is the account of scientific archeologists that denies the authenticity of the "human" footprints while recognizing the significance of the dinosaur tracks. Their account has its followers and is set within the framework of the vast body of modern biology, geology, and anthropology. Which account is accurate? Which of these or other accounts is authentic? Which is best?

To answer those and similar questions, it is helpful to view the various archeologies as consisting of various sets of rules that must be followed if a satisfactory account of the past is to be produced. Then the questions can be answered in terms of how well the rules are followed in constructing a particular account. In the example, the apparent contradiction between the two accounts can be resolved. Assuming the rules underlying each were equally well observed, the accounts have equal accuracy and authenticity, and the best is the one most believable to those who accept the rules for constructing that account. Given several accounts that follow the same rules, the best would be the one constructed with the most care that the rules were followed. Thus, the account offered by religious archeology has little merit, because although it observes some of the rules of conventional religion and some of the rules of conventional science, it does neither well. An interesting aspect of this view of archeology is the idea that a particular account of the past may provide more insight into the culture, the mental processes, of those who accept it than it provides about people of the past.

I am a scientific archeologist. I have been trained in the conventional scientific tradition, the tradition that provides the basis for most technical and popular archeological accounts in this country. I know a little about other traditions, and as an anthropologist, I understand them but do not advocate them.

The purpose of this section is to present some of the concepts, theories, methods, and techniques (the rules) of scientific archeology. Since this book is a guide, the presentation here is necessarily brief and selective. Readers who would like to pursue these and other ideas in greater depth will find useful suggestions in the annotated list of references at the end of this chapter.

Basically, there are two major aspects of modern scientific archeology: the archeological record and the interpretation of the archeological record. It would simplify things if the two were independent of one another, but they are not. They are so interrelated that it is not possible to untangle them completely. For purposes of discussion, however, it is useful to distinguish between these conceptual areas.

The Archeological Record

The archeological record consists of evidence of the past, known and unknown, recorded and unrecorded, recognized and unrecognized, perceived and unperceived. In short, it is *all* evidence of the past. It is evidence of the natural environment (sometimes called ecofacts) as well as the cultural environment (artifacts). Archeologists direct much of their effort toward the discovery and the recording of evidence of the past. Discovery usually involves site survey and excavation; recording involves the compilation and maintenance not only of the objects themselves but also of all manner of associations related to the objects.

Discovery: Site Survey and Excavation

For most people the most exciting part of archeology involves the adventure and romance of discovery. We like to "walkabout" in search of artifacts, hunting for sites as though we were playing the role of Indiana Jones in the movie *Raiders of the Lost Ark*. Site survey is that part of discovery that involves the location and tabulation of sites, and excavation is just that: digging.

A typical site survey or excavation has three phases: preliminary investigation; fieldwork, or the search; and description, analysis, and reporting (the recording of the evidence). As in any process, the phases are interrelated and dependent upon one another, yet each represents a distinctive set of activities that must be followed in the order listed for maximum effectiveness.

Preliminary investigation. The objective of this phase is to learn as much as possible about what is to be done. Although it may seem obvious, it is especially important at the outset to be clear about exactly what is to be done. If, for example, the problem is to discover as many archeological sites as possible in a given area, the procedures (operating under the ever-present restraints of time and money) might be considerably different from what they would be if the problem were merely that of finding a specific kind of site. Although discovery should begin with a clear statement of what is to be accomplished, the archeologist can change such a statement as the work progresses.

The basic procedure of this phase is to formulate a game plan, a scheme to guide the work. It starts with the study of all literature (published and unpublished reports, articles, monographs, field notes, maps, photographs) directly related to the known archeological record of the work to be done. That is a necessary minimum and often requires an extensive and time-consuming records check. Additional background research should include information about the geography, geology, history, and anthropology of the target area. Ideally, the initial game plan should be couched in terms of some theoretical perspective, such as the idea of social and cultural (sociocultural) evolution discussed in the next chapter.

Keeping in mind that the purpose of preliminary work is to prepare logistically as well as conceptually, the archeologist must study such items as property ownership maps, transportation requirements, and possible means of communication. As part of the logistical preliminaries, it is especially important to obtain the necessary permits to perform the work in question. If the permits are not obtained, the entire project is jeopardized and may prove untenable. It is best to solve this problem as early as possible.

Fieldwork: the search. This is usually the most satisfying part of the discovery process. For most people who have been in the field searching for sites or plumbing the depths of a site at a dig, the rewards (or punishments, depending on individual preference) of the work itself—hiking, experiencing the various sensory pleasures of the outdoors, feeling a little adventuresome—are incidental to the thrill of discovery. The degree to which one is able to follow the game plan and not be led astray by the rigors of discovery is a sign of maturity as an archeologist.

Fieldwork consists of a personal, physical, on-site search according to the plan formulated during the preliminary phase. Orientation is one of the most pervasive problems encountered during site survey and excavation. Not only is there the constant possibility of getting lost during a survey, but there is also the basic need to record the location of those sites found. In areas for which modern maps or aerial photographs are available, the problem is greatly simplified. Besides maps, data concerning sites are typically recorded in various media including field notes, photographs, and even video recordings. When necessary and justified, samples may be systematically collected.

Orientation is especially critical in excavation where the location of important finds must be marked with great accuracy. There are a variety of methods. Most of them require preparation of a detailed map of the site based on an arbitrarily determined reference (datum) point. Discoveries are then oriented with reference to that point.

Excavation is the most widely known, popularly identified aspect of archeology. It is far and away the most labor-intensive aspect of the discipline and often involves moving tons of earth. It can be extremely boring as well as intensely thrilling and includes the least skillful as well as the most skillful combinations of intellect, intuition, and hand-eye coordination. A good "shovel bum" is as crucial to the successful completion of a dig as the presence of a competent concertmaster is to the performance of a symphony.

For the job to be done well, a site must be excavated in a systematic way to facilitate later description and interpretation. In all archeological discovery, the purpose of excavation is not merely the discovery and collection of objects but also the discovery and systematic collection of information about the context within which the objects are found.

It is a rule-of-thumb that sites should be excavated in such a way that if necessary, they can be fully restored. The rule is useful to emphasize the importance of careful excavation and detailed recording, but in practice it is downright silly. No site is excavated with complete restoration in mind. If not impossible, it at least is quite improbable that a site could be restored to a pre-excavated condition. Sites are excavated for preconceived reasons developed in essentially the same phases as those described for site survey.

Although the intricacies of fieldwork are beyond the scope of this book, the interested reader can consult any of the several outstanding books listed at the end of this chapter for further orientation concerning the conventions of archeological fieldwork. It is important to know about the difficulties of fieldwork in order to appreciate the sites described here.

These sites are especially significant because most of the unpleasant aspects of discovery have been eliminated, while some of the most satisfying aspects remain.

One thing to contemplate in visiting these sites is the intensity of modern effort required to find and record them, to excavate and interpret them, and to prepare and preserve them. In many ways those efforts are as remarkable as the cultures the sites are thought to represent.

Recording the Evidence

The recording of evidence is perhaps the least understood and most troublesome part of archeology. Although the excitement, interest, and intense emotions of archeology are usually manifest in the discovery of the material objects—the artifacts and the sites—the all-important key to understanding the objects lies in recording their association to one another and to the contexts within which they were found.

Recording is usually neither glamorous nor exciting but is often routine and repetitive. It is just plain hard work, yet it is what preserves the associations, the context, and enhances the meaning of the objects, a meaning that far transcends the significance of the objects themselves. Each individual object, removed from its context, is like any part separated from the whole: it is stripped of its meaning. The old saying holds true—"The whole is greater than the sum of its parts."

For example, when one finds an arrowhead and picks it up, that object is removed from the context within which it was found. If that context is not systematically preserved, it is lost forever. Although a single arrowhead, by itself, may not be of great significance, it is vital that the collector be aware of the loss each time it occurs. Through time and the efforts of thousands of collectors, the loss is multiplied until it becomes overwhelming. Undocumented relic collecting is one of the most serious threats to the archeological record and is strongly discouraged.

Individuals who are interested in acquiring the skills necessary for recording archeological data might consider participating in field schools sponsored by the Texas Archeological Society, a college or university, or some other organization that supervises and mentors students

and allows them to practice recording skills and techniques. Fieldwork can be learned properly only in the field.

Interpretation of the
Archeological Record

If the archeological record is seen as any type of evidence of the past, then how the record is to be interpreted becomes an important factor in the discovery and
recording of that evidence. The game plan an archeologist develops during preliminary research is intended to
control the process of discovery and recording. Old say-
ings in science for this situation are "The question is the
important thing; the answers will follow," or "The solution to the problem lies in how the question is asked."
Thus, as pointed out earlier, the archeological record and
the interpretation of that record are so intertwined that
an intended interpretation becomes significant in determining the nature of the record.

Turning from that rather obscure but extremely important relationship, let us consider the matter of interpretation in a more conventional sense. How can we tell what
it means?

The answer depends to a large extent on the kind of
archeology one is practicing. In the past few decades archeology has developed a great diversity, paralleling the
increasing specialization characteristic of society in
general. Today there are specializations such as historical
archeology, industrial archeology, behavioral archeology, garbageology, prehistoric archeology, anthropological
archeology, Old World archeology, New World archeology, Classical archeology, nautical archeology, and experimental archeology. Of course there is a great deal
of overlap among the specialties. In practice an archeologist is apt to use ideas from any specialty when it comes
to discovering and interpreting data from the past. Still,
there is a conscious sorting into the various specialties,
a fragmentation reflected in the names and number of
special-interest associations within archeology. Whatever
the specialization, the problem of the transformation of

the archeological record is universal. By "transformation," I simply mean that the archeological record must be transformed, literally changed in form, from one state into another.

Take, for example, the problem of establishing a temporal sequence. Often referred to as chronology, or simply dating, it is the major problem in archeology. A discipline that is principally concerned with formulating accounts of the past must have some way to relate that past to the present. It is of crucial importance to develop a set of conventions, techniques, that prescribe the rules governing the transformation of the archeological record from one form to another. One such technique is the transformation of lumps of charcoal into a number that represents a date.

The process includes the proper selection of the samples of charcoal for dating, the treatment of the samples, and the evaluation of the results of the treatment. Each step is governed by more or less explicit rules that delineate the proper procedure for this type of dating. A good carbon date is one that has been determined after close adherence to that procedure. The remainder of this section presents some of the basic rules for determining dates in archeology. These dating techniques are general models of all rules of interpretation in archeology.

Of the many techniques of dating, only a few, usually those most often used, are considered here. It is conventional, although misleading, to divide the techniques into those that yield specific dates, called absolute dating techniques, and those called relative dating techniques, which simply allow events to be arranged in sequence without reference to specific units of time.

At first, the difference between the two kinds of dating may seem a little confusing. To keep them straight it helps to think of time as a bottomless well, and we in the present are standing on the ground at the top of the well. If we throw a rope over the edge and go down into the well, we are traveling back in time. If we have no way of measuring how deeply we have descended into the well, we have no way of knowing how far we have traveled in time. This is similar to relative dating. As we descend into time we know we are farther into the past, relative to the previous stage of descent, but we don't know how much farther.

If, however, we tie knots in the rope at regular intervals—one-foot intervals would be convenient—we can tell how deep we have descended into the well simply by counting the knots. We can tell with some confidence when we have descended eight feet, ten feet, fifteen feet, and so on. This is like absolute dating. When we go back through time, we can assign a unit of time to each stage, in much the same way we assign a unit of distance to each depth in the well.

The relative dating techniques to be discussed are stratigraphy, fluorine analysis, pollen analysis, and seriation. Absolute techniques include historic methods, radiocarbon dating, dendrochronology, and archeomagnetism. Each is illustrated at one or more of the sites discussed in this book.

Relative Dating Techniques
Stratigraphy. This is without doubt the most important method of dating prehistoric sites. It is used to establish relationships in all kinds of archeology, but in prehistoric archeology it has no peer.

The concept of stratigraphy is quite simple. Sometimes referred to as the rule or law of superposition, it states simply that when a thing is covered by something else, the lower thing had to be there first. In everyday terms, when you make up your bed in the morning, you cover the bed with sheets, place pillows on the sheets, and cover everything with a bedspread. Following the rule of superposition, anyone who found your bed, assuming it hadn't been severely disturbed, could determine that the bed was there first, the sheets were placed on the bed before the pillows, then the pillows were put in place, and finally the bedspread covered the pillows and the rest.

But wait. You may point out that some people put the bedspread on before the pillows, then turn it down at the head and insert the pillows. Well, that's true. Nobody declares that stratigraphy (or any dating technique) is perfect; it's just the best we can do at present.

The techniques of stratigraphic analysis were developed in the early nineteenth century in England and Scotland by the founders of modern geology. If you have ever been to the Grand Canyon, you have seen a classic example of the massive stratigraphic deposits geologists have to work with. In such huge formations, problems of the pillow-bedspread type, although still potentially misleading, are relatively easy to catch in comparison with the small stratigraphic distinctions typical in archeology. Because of the small scale of the strata studied by archeologists, such study is often referred to as microstratigraphy.

Stratigraphy has been a major concept in the development of modern geology and archeology and has been used in dating every site described here. Some of the uses, difficulties, and variations of stratigraphic technique are clearly illustrated in the sections on Lubbock Lake, the Clovis Site, and Fort Davis.

Fluorine analysis. This is one of several techniques that depend upon chemical analysis. Fluorine analysis derives from the same kind of observations that led to the inclusion of fluorine in modern water supply systems, including observations of populations such as those at Turkey, Texas, where there is a high percentage of fluorine in the groundwater. It was discovered that fluorine will replace certain chemicals in bone, making the bone harder and teeth more resistant to decay, and that's why fluorine is added to drinking water.

That knowledge became useful as a dating technique when it was realized that bones of the same age and buried in the same deposit should, all else being equal, have about the same amount of fluorine in them. Measuring and comparing the amounts of fluorine in the bones should determine their age relative to one another.

There are many problems with this technique. Most of them have to do with the assumption that a difference in fluorine content reflects a difference in age. As it turns out, only in a few circumstances can it be assumed that all other things are equal.

One place where this technique has been used to good effect is the Scharbauer Site (sometimes referred to as the Midland Site) near Midland. Although the site is not easily accessible and so is not described in this book, it produced remains that are among the earliest known human skeletal materials in the New World. Fluorine analysis was used to good advantage to reinforce the apparent stratigraphic association of the human remains with remains of Pleistocene animals.

Pollen analysis. Pollen analysis (palynology) has been used not only for dating but also for reconstructing past climates. The technique, although rather simple in concept, is difficult in application.

As is widely known today, many plants produce pollen during their reproductive cycle. The physical characteristics of pollen are species specific; that is, based on such observable features as shape, size, color, and density, pollen can be clearly identified with the type of plant that produced it. Pollen can be just as accurate an indicator as leaves or fruit in matters of plant identification. That is how the TV weatherman is able to report what kinds of plants are responsible for the allergies of the day.

Furthermore, the plants growing in an area are clearly related to the climatic conditions of that area. A pollen analyst can distinguish a sample of desert plant pollen from a sample of rain forest pollen as easily as most people can tell the difference between a cactus and a Christmas tree. It is relatively easy, in concept at least, to determine variations in the climate at a site simply by analyzing pollen samples representing different periods at that site. The climatic variations at one site can then serve as a basis for correlating similar climatic variations at another site.

Although the technique is more tedious and the results more tenuous than this brief characterization suggests, pollen analysis can be quite useful. Archeologists have used it successfully at a number of sites in Texas. The

Clovis Site and the Lubbock Lake Site are good examples of its value in dating and climatic reconstruction.

Seriation. The principle of seriation is the same as that of evolution, growth, or development. It views change as the process of accumulation of small differences through time. When we plant a cucumber seed, we can expect eventually to have cucumbers. This does not happen immediately but rather reflects the accumulation of small differences in the process of cucumber development. Starting with the planting of the seed, distinct, recognizable stages in that development include flowering, emergence of first leaf, harvest of first cucumber, swelling and rupture of seed, rapid growth of vine, and appearance of plant aboveground. As anyone familiar with plant development knows, those stages are not listed in developmental sequence. That is, they are not in chronological, or serial, order.

Similarly, anyone familiar with the concept of seriation would recognize that the events are not in serial order, even if that person knows nothing about cucumber or plant growth. Simply stated, a developmental series will show a direct relationship between the similarity of objects (or events) and their closeness in time. Thus, an object that is similar to another object in the same series is nearer to it in time than to some very different thing in the series.

To return to our cucumber garden. If we start with one stage, emergence of first leaf, for example, and compare it with all other stages, it will be most like two other stages, in this case appearance of plant aboveground and rapid growth of vine. Placing those stages adjacent to the stage of emergence of first leaf, we have: rapid growth of vine, emergence of first leaf, and appearance of plant aboveground. If we compare the first and last with the remaining stages, the seriation grows to: flowering, rapid growth of vine, emergence of first leaf, appearance of plant aboveground, and swelling and rupture of seed. Continuing the process, we end up with this developmental seriation: harvest of first cucumber, flowering, rapid growth of vine, emergence of first leaf, appearance of plant aboveground, swelling and rupture of seed, and planting of seed. All this is possible without knowing about cucumbers, but it is necessary to know the principle of seriation.

Of course, people who know about cucumbers know that the sequence is reversed; we don't harvest before we plant. The technique doesn't allow researchers to determine which is the earliest end of the sequence; it merely helps them arrange items in developmental sequence. They must rely on some other source for information about which end of the sequence is earliest.

The principle of seriation may be applied in any situation when a developmental sequence can be assumed. One of the most widely employed techniques, it is used to date sites, artifacts, and even entire cultures. The sequence of stages, or periods, often used in standard archeological interpretation relies in part on the concept of development of cultures through time (cultural evolution) and, therefore, on the concept of seriation.

Absolute Dating Techniques

Historic dating. This is a form of dating we are all familiar with. In archeology it is often based on the association of objects of known date of manufacture with other objects of unknown date. When used in conjunction with stratigraphy or some other method of establishing associations, it is the best dating technique. As with all these techniques, however, it must be used with caution.

Radiocarbon dating. More than all the other dating techniques, radioactive carbon dating (C^{14}, carbon 14, radiocarbon) has captured the public imagination. It is in a paradoxical position as one of the most useful and, at the same time, one of the most easily misused of the techniques for dating. It is useful because it provides an independent check of dating efforts, a fail-safe mechanism that tells archeologists when they are on the right track and when their relative chronologies are way off. If, for example, a researcher has established a sequence by seriation, but the dates derived from radioactive carbon associated with the end of the sequence are consistently earlier than those at the middle, the researcher would need to look again at the seriation. More commonly, radiocarbon dating is considered important because it remains the most reliable, easiest, and least expensive absolute technique for dating prehistoric sites.

Radiocarbon dating can be misused in a variety of ways. Some are technical problems—of sampling, laboratory procedures, and interpretation—and might occur even with the best of intentions. Often, however, the results of radiocarbon dating are deliberately misused. Such distortion, which is a barely concealed form of lying, is not practiced by responsible archeologists in Texas or elsewhere, but it is common among authors of sensational books claiming, for example, an extraterrestrial origin for humanity.

The principle behind radiocarbon dating is quite simple. A tiny amount of the common element carbon occurs in a radioactive form known as carbon 14. Radioactive forms (isotopes) such as carbon 14 lose their radioactivity at a rate typical for that isotope. That rate of decay is usually indicated by the amount of time required for a given sample to lose half its radioactivity (the radioactive half-life). In the case of carbon 14, the half-life is approximately 5,800 years, meaning that a sample of radioactive carbon could be expected to emit only half as much radioactivity in 5,800 years as it does today. By the same token, a sample today could be expected to have only half as much radioactivity as it had about 5,800 years ago, one fourth as much as 11,600 years ago, and so on.

This technique assumes that the amount of radioactivity measured in a sample of carbon is a valid indicator of its age. Usually, substances such as charcoal (the favorite sample material), wood, or other formerly living organic material are preferred, since such material supposedly incurs no new carbon 14 after the death of the organism, and the carbon 14 in the system will decay at the typical rate.

Radiocarbon dates have been obtained for various

aspects of almost all sites mentioned in this book. Such dates have been particularly well explored in the work at Caddoan Mounds.

Dendrochronology. This is a big word for tree-ring dating. It is based on the observation that many kinds of trees produce annual growth rings. The dark part of the rings represents the time of the year when the tree was dormant, the winter perhaps. The light part of the rings represents the big, abundant cells characteristic of a period of rapid growth. Thus, in these trees, the number of rings is roughly equivalent to the age of the tree. All years are not equally favorable for tree growth, however. In years of favorable conditions, the tree rings will be substantially different from those formed when growth is stunted. Trees in a region tend to experience a similar, regional pattern of growth cycles. It is possible to correlate the distinctive patterns of ring growth in living and dead trees and thereby extend the pattern through time. The long-range pattern of tree-ring variation is the fundamental tool of dendrochronology. Although archeologists have tried to use dendrochronology on several occasions in Texas, it has seldom produced good results here. It has been used successfully in Arizona and other areas of the desert Southwest, however, and will perhaps yet prove more useful in Texas.

Archeomagnetism. This is one of the least-used methods of dating. An unusual and stringent set of conditions must be met before it is feasible. Even then, the dates produced are tenuous.

The technique relies on a well-known phenomenon, the wandering of the magnetic poles; that is, magnetic north is not fixed. It seems to wander about the axis of the earth's rotation, and the course of its wanderings has been plotted using historical records. When iron-bearing materials, such as many kinds of clay, are heated above a certain temperature (the Curie point), the iron is aligned, compasslike, toward magnetic north. If the material has not been moved since it was heated, researchers may be able to determine when it was heated by determining the dates when iron would have aligned with the pole in that direction. Pottery kilns, lava, bricks, and fire hearths have been dated using this technique, but it has been attempted at several sites in Texas with only limited success. Data for possible use of the technique were obtained at the Lewisville Site.

As the above outline of dating concerns and techniques illustrates, the concept of transformation is simply a rather self-conscious version of interpretation. In essence, interpretation is the following of rules that allow transformation of the archeological record from one form into another. In the case of radiocarbon dating, for example, certain rules specify the characteristics of acceptable samples, other rules dictate how those samples must be treated, and still other rules determine how the results are presented. The value of a particular interpretation can be judged by how well the rules for arriving at that interpretation were followed.

If this all seems confusing, just consider that the training a person undergoes to become an archeologist (or a dentist, a homemaker, an auto mechanic, or any learned human activity) consists of learning the rules of that occupation. Somewhat more complex rules are demonstrated in the following chapter on sociocultural evolution.

Further Reading

Any of the following would make an excellent starting point for understanding the conventional rules of developing and interpreting the archeological record.

Ashmore, W., and R. J. Sharer. 1988. *Discovering Our Past.* Mount View, California: Mayfield. This new paperback provides an inexpensive, general introduction to the conventions of modern archeology. There are many similarly good introductory books on the subject; this is merely one of the most recent.

Hester, Thomas R. 1980. *Digging Into South Texas Prehistory: A Guide for Amateur Archaeologists.* San Antonio: Corona. Written by a native South Texan who is also professor of anthropology at the University of

Texas, this book manages to be both authoritative and informal in presentation. Many of the ideas that are presented and illustrated within the context of South Texas sites are easily extended to other parts of the state. Highly recommended.

Hester, Thomas R., Robert F. Heizer, and John A. Graham. 1975. *Field Methods in Archaeology,* 6th edition. Palo Alto, California: Mayfield. One of the most popular of all field texts, this edition includes many examples from Texas. A classic, useful book. Highly recommended.

Joukowsky, Martha. 1980. *A Complete Manual of Field Archaeology: Tools and Techniques of Field Work for Archaeologists.* Englewood Cliffs, New Jersey: Prentice-Hall. This is a comprehensive guide to field archeology. Recommended.

Oakley, K. P. 1964. *Frameworks for Dating Fossil Man.* Chicago: Aldine. Although out of date in many respects, this remains one of the most quoted sources for dating techniques—a classic of its type.

3
Social and Cultural Evolution

Evolution is one of the major concepts underlying modern anthropological interpretation. This section will explain some of the basic concepts of cultural evolution and how they relate to archeology in general and, especially, archeology in Texas.

Basically, evolution is simply a means of explaining change through time; it is seen as the gradual accumulation of small increments until change becomes noticeable. Since evolution is a continuous process of accumulation, generally from relatively simple to relatively complex forms, it is conventional to break the process into discrete units for purposes of description and analysis. For example, when we describe the development of a human being from birth to death, an evolutionary journey through life, it is conventional to divide the continuous process of living a life into such stages as neonate, infant, toddler, child, adolescent, and so on. Although these stages of development, or evolution, can be defined and compared with one another, we realize that they are at least somewhat arbitrary and that they must be used with their inherent limitations in mind.

One of the limitations most apparent in archeology is that the societies and cultures we can observe and describe are all as recent as their ethnographic history. They are as recent as we are. They represent the most recent expression of their own social and cultural development and have changed through time to an unknown, and perhaps unknowable, degree. Furthermore, both the rate and the continuity of change are unknown. To formulate a scheme of social and cultural evolution based on modern, contemporaneous societies is analogous to formulating a scheme of human development based on a cross section of contemporaneous persons. If we could not test our scheme of human development by watching babies grow into adulthood, such a scheme might be extremely misleading. Even with the opportunity to test by observation, theories of human development are controversial. The situation is even more tenuous in archeology, because our histories aren't long enough to serve as a test for a particular idea of how societies and cultures evolve.

Therefore, when we develop evolutionary schemes using ethnographic data, it is important to remember that the stages thus derived are but tentative models and are subject to change. Indeed, perhaps the strongest argument for the significance of archeological data is that such data provide the best known body of information to test our ideas concerning sociocultural change.

Recent schemes of sociocultural evolution are usually based, in part, on means of subsistence. By "subsistence" is meant the characteristic way the people of a society obtain the necessities of life, that is, how they make a living. Subsistence-based models are among the most widely used and the most useful for archeological interpretation, because they can be correlated with material objects that last through time. Alternative schemes based on more ephemeral cultural traits such as kinship, rules of marriage, or other aspects of social organization have not proven as useful to archeologists.

Stages drawn from the ethnographic record and based on type of subsistence include hunting and gathering, early food production, and agriculture. Additional, more-complex stages have been proposed, but those three seem to be sufficient to account for most of the archeology of Texas.

The stages are discussed below in terms of:

Subsistence. This term refers to the manner of deriving the necessities of life, the economy.

Geographic extent. The area occupied by the society, its territory.

Settlement pattern. The manner of distribution of the population of a society in its geographic area.

Architecture. Emphasis here is on the built environment, especially new forms of construction seen as characteristic of each stage.

Type of exchange. The exchange of wealth, trade.

The Hunting and Gathering Stage

This stage of social and cultural evolution is represented at most prehistoric archeological sites in Texas. Understanding the significance of that fact is crucial to any insight into the interpretation of the archeological record of the state.

Surprisingly, current ideas concerning life in hunting and gathering societies are in many ways contradictory to the ideas widely held by anthropologists until about thirty years ago. At that time they began to realize that their picture of hunters and gatherers had been unduly biased because most of what they knew of this way of life had been derived from observation of groups whose culture had been influenced to some degree by contact with food-producing peoples. People in hunting and gathering societies were believed to be so caught up in the daily struggle for existence—tending to basic needs such as food, clothing, and shelter—that they were prevented from advancing to higher forms of culture. Today we know that isn't necessarily so. Instead, many such societies are characterized by large amounts of leisure time. Lack of development is now seen as an indicator of cultural conservatism, a resistance to change known as ethnocentrism.

With the realization that all people in all parts of the world lived in hunting and gathering societies until about 12,000 years ago came the realization that the best way to test our ideas concerning life in such societies is through archeology. Archeological techniques are the only way we have to derive data concerning the way of life, the culture, of people in "pure" hunting and gathering societies.

In light of the new emphasis on hunting and gathering societies, the archeology of Texas becomes especially important. Sites that formerly were considered to be "just another campsite" or "one more hearth" now are seen to have great potential in providing information to test our ideas of life in hunting and gathering societies. For example, the exclusive presence of hunting and gathering societies in South Texas at the time of earliest historic contact led some anthropologists to use the term "culture sink" to describe the situation in that area. Although it is true that sociocultural evolution there remained at a hunting and gathering stage of subsistence until most recently, the negative tone of the term "culture sink" is unwarranted. Instead, the hunting and gathering societies of South Texas are seen as successful, conservative survivors in an increasingly restricted environment. The examination of their sites offers an excellent opportunity to study the culture of hunters and gatherers in a world without food production.

Texas is rich with potential for the study of such societies and the culture associated with them. To try to grasp the cultural dynamics of societies without food-producing subsistence, let us look at some characteristic features of hunting and gathering societies.

Subsistence. Hunting and gathering societies, also known as foraging or extractive societies, are most easily identified as all those societies that depend entirely on wild or undomesticated species for food. That is, they have no domesticated plants or animals that are used directly for food. Many hunting and gathering societies have domestic dogs, but they are not primarily for food.

In some ways the terms "foraging" and "extractive" are preferable to "hunting and gathering," since they are more general and do not sound as though they exclude entrapping, shellfish collecting, fishing, and other techniques. Nevertheless, "hunting and gathering" is pretty well established in the literature, and I will continue to use it here with the understanding that it includes all manner of food procurement that does not directly entail species domesticated for food.

Geographic extent. All societies occupy a geographic area. In the case of hunting and gathering societies, the area tends to be relatively small. Although the boundaries between adjacent groups may be as clearly delineated as a stream bank, much more often such bounds are so vaguely defined that the people themselves may have no concept of territoriality at all but think of themselves simply as following migrations of some animal species.

Since the area in which a hunting and gathering group lives must furnish most of the resources necessary for survival, members of the group typically have detailed knowledge of plants, animals, topography, and other environmental features. The culture of the group reflects those natural features. If one knows what natural resources are available in an area, it becomes relatively simple to spot imported items.

Settlement pattern. Population size and density in these societies are both low. Such societies are small, seldom more than 500 people, and the number of persons per unit of land area (population density) is very low, characteristically in the range of one person per square mile. For contrast, consider that Texas today has a population density of about 60 persons per square mile for the state as a whole and about 1,450 per square mile for Harris County, the state's most populous county.

People in hunting and gathering societies usually live in several small, local groups of kinsmen. Although they tend to be related through a male lineage, necessity seems to be more significant than lineage in determining where a person will live. Within the limits provided by their area, the people are seminomadic and follow the cycle of maturing resources in their movements from place to place.

Architecture. As one might expect, the built environment in such groups is minimal. Various instances of ethnographic archeology (ethnography with archeological interpretation in mind) have revealed little evidence that survived as brief a period as a few months after occupation. Generally, temporary shelters, hearths, windscreens, and similar constructions of a rather ephemeral nature are associated with hunters and gatherers. Occasionally, however, much more substantial architecture is encountered in such societies.

Type of exchange. Although there are exceptions, people in hunting and gathering societies tend to be of the same social class; that is, such societies are egalitarian and are characterized by leveling mechanisms that maintain a relatively equal distribution of wealth. One of the most effective of those devices is a type of exchange in which individuals, upon obtaining wealth, share it with others with no specific expectation of repayment. This type of exchange, sometimes referred to as general reciprocity, results in a more or less free exchange throughout the area occupied by a group. Practically the only concentration of resources is dictated by local availability and the location of campsites. In short, there are relatively few trade items.

The Early Food Production Stage

The advent of a symbiotic relationship between human beings and other species marked one of the most profound transformations in human social and cultural evolution. The transformation has been called the Neolithic Revolution because of the truly immense effect the transition from hunting and gathering to food production has had on the reality of human existence. The effects of the transition on patterns of subsistence are extensive.

Subsistence. A major shift in artifacts from types associated with hunting and gathering to types associated with food production technology is most useful in determining early domestication on the basis of archeological remains. Besides the usual artifacts associated with hunting and gathering—projectile points and other stone tools, snares, baskets—early food producers frequently have bone and stone tools for cultivation; storage facilities such as baskets, pottery, and storerooms; grinding tools such as mortars and pestles, manos and metates; as well as the domesticates themselves. Earliest forms of pottery often appear early in the development of food production technology, although pottery itself is not an infallible indicator of domestication.

Worldwide, the archeological record indicates that certain shifts in the hardware of food production actually precede or at least accompany the shift in subsistence. Similarly, although the shift has been termed a revolution, evidence indicates the transformation may have required more time than the term "revolution" normally implies. This stage represents a time in which hunting and gathering is gradually phased out and is replaced by increasing dependence on domesticated varieties.

In terms of significance to Texas archeology, one of the most exciting possibilities, as yet unrealized, is the discovery of very early domesticates somewhere in the state. In general, the conditions seem to be right, but so far no convincing evidence has been reported.

Geographic extent. The geographic range of early food-producing societies is small in comparison with other societies with different forms of subsistence. These societies, however, remain similar to hunting and gathering societies in terms of the size of area exploited. Generally, there is an inverse relationship between the degree of dependence on domesticated species and the size of the area the society occupies: the greater the dependence, the smaller the area. Boundaries tend to be more stable and clearly defined as the degree of dependence on food production increases. Therefore, a well-established early food-producing society with relatively little dependence on hunting and gathering would be expected to occupy a fairly small, clearly bounded area.

Settlement pattern. One of the distinct shifts that occurs in the transformation from hunting and gathering to food production is the change from a nomadic, cyclic existence characteristic of hunters and gatherers to the sedentary existence characteristic of most food producers. The population of early food producers is larger and the population density is greater than is typical of hunters and gatherers. Most of the people live in or near small, continuously occupied villages.

Architecture. In the earlier stages of food production, the houses are single-room structures but tend to be constructed with more rooms as the complexity of the society increases. Increasing social complexity is correlated with an increase in architectural specialization in other ways. Gradually, buildings dedicated to a specific purpose begin to be built, and the structure of the village itself reflects the specialization characteristic of increasing social complexity. For example, some buildings are larger than others. Artifacts associated with these buildings reinforce the idea that they serve some special purpose such as religious ritual and provide a focal point for the community.

Type of exchange. Along with increasing specialization in the built environment, there is a shift in the form of exchange from one of generalized exchange to a balanced exchange in which some goods or services are exchanged for others of equal value. Trade is more widespread, and centers of trade, marketplaces, are characteristic. The sedentary villages collect materials from a wide area, and many of the specialized structures are related to the exchange and production of wealth. Not only are objects from far away found in these villages, but locally produced goods are traded regionally as well.

The Agriculture Stage

This stage is noted for full agricultural production, and there is little dependence on hunting and gathering. (Although in North America turkeys were the major source of domesticated animal protein and wild species were used for certain protein foods, hunting still became relatively unimportant among peoples at this stage of development.) Social and cultural forces unleashed by discoveries of new technologies continue to bring wave after wave of change, and societies at this level of evolution tend to be very unstable.

Although culture developed far greater complexity elsewhere in North America, this stage of development marks the zenith of prehistoric evolution in Texas. Other areas in North America, most particularly in the southwestern states of Arizona, New Mexico, Colorado, and Utah as well as portions of the Mississippi drainage (particularly the American Bottoms at Cahokia), and various localities in Mexico proceeded to more complex societies, but cultures in Texas were at this or less complex levels of sociocultural evolution at the time of their earliest contact with the Western European tradition.

Subsistence. As mentioned above, subsistence technology becomes quite sophisticated during this stage. Crop rotation, irrigation, use of fertilizers, improved species, and new techniques of storage and cultivation are introduced, and new methods of tilling the fields and bringing new land into production are characteristic advances. Other new technologies often correlated with full agricultural production include improved pottery for storage and cooking, new cooking techniques including ovens for baking dough products, and systems of notation (precursors of writing and computation) for recording seasonal cycles.

Geographic extent. The area dominated by an advanced agricultural society can be quite extensive, with considerable variation in cultural expression. This type of dominance is, in many respects, similar to variation in modern societies. In modern Texas, for example, influences from a major urban center such as Dallas are felt throughout the state, even though individuals may be living a rural, rather isolated, existence. So it is in societies at an agricultural stage of development. They extend throughout a region and are often bounded by other, similar societies with whom they compete for territory and resources. People in remote, outlying zones often find themselves first in one and then in another larger sociocultural group. Under such conditions, boundaries between competing groups are tenuous and subject to repeated change. As the boundaries change, so the area changes, waxing and waning in harmony with the relative fortunes of the various competing societies.

Settlement pattern. The populations of full agricultural societies are typically larger than preceding populations. Rapid population growth is one facet of success in food-producing technology; such societies abruptly increase in size and, in the process, splinter, colonize, and continue their rapid growth in new locales. This factor is correlated with growth in area, as discussed above.

In addition to a marked increase in population size,

these societies can develop and maintain a relatively high population density. The villages that are characteristic of early food-producing societies become larger, their numbers are greater, and a few become large, densely populated centers for regional transactions including production and distribution of wealth, governance, and entertainment. A highly differentiated class structure is characteristic, and the major regional centers are the home base for the ruling elite.

Architecture. Major works requiring the coordinated efforts of large numbers of people are characteristic of this level of development. They are both a function of and made possible by the size and density of population. For example, societies at this stage construct large earth mounds as a base for temples, as burial mounds, or for functions unknown. Extensive irrigation systems, communication networks for trade and information exchange, as well as large public monuments and other structures are established and maintained. Differences in social class are reflected in architecture in numerous ways, such as the obvious differences in size, complexity, style, and location of residential structures. In addition there are clear class differences in burial practices and funerary offerings.

Areas of the larger settlements come to reflect an increased specialization and fragmentation of the society and become distinguished by new forms of interdependence. Some areas reflect a preoccupation with trade, others with production (pottery, basketry, stone tools, works of art, for example), and still other areas are associated with religion, governance, and accumulation of technological knowledge. All those variations have expressions in the built environment.

Type of exchange. Trade in this stage is extensive. To a significant extent, population centers are centers of commerce, and the larger settlements become the focus for large quantities of products, both locally produced and brought from vast distances.

A new kind of exchange is manifest in these centers. In this type of exchange, unlike previous systems in which value was balanced, value is no longer equal. Each exchange tends to represent a transaction in which something of value, food for example, is exchanged for something of no intrinsic value, such as money. A true market economy is thus characteristic of this stage.

Further Reading

The following references may be consulted for further, more-detailed discussion of ethnography, ethnology, and social and cultural evolution. Most are readily available in local bookstores and libraries.

Childe, V. G. 1951. *Social Evolution.* London: Watts. Professor Childe's books were among the most widely read, popular works dealing with social and cultural evolution of his time. Although outdated in terms of specific information and technique, they are still essentially sound in terms of concept and execution. I have found this one especially helpful.

Harris, M. 1979. *Cultural Materialism.* New York: Thomas Y. Crowell. This book represents one of the best, most comprehensive discussions of the interrelationship between systems of production and cultural and social evolution. It is quite extensive and requires dedication to read through—not for the casual reader.

Newcomb, W. W., Jr. 1961. *The Indians of Texas From Prehistoric to Modern Times.* Austin: University of Texas Press. After more than a quarter century, this remains the most comprehensive single source of ethnographic information concerning Native Americans in Texas. It is useful in many ways and is recommended to anyone with interest in the anthropology of this region.

Nunley, Parker. 1972. Toward a generalized model of hunting and gathering societies. *Bulletin of the Texas Archeological Society* 43:13–31. This is a more detailed, technical description of hunters and gatherers than the one in the current chapter, with a good bibliography of hunting and gathering societies up until about 1969.

Service, E. R. 1978. *Profiles in Ethnology.* New York: Harper and Row. A classic example of the combination of particular, ethnographic description and cultural evolution, this includes ethnographic summaries of 25 cultures ranging from the hunting and gathering Arunta of central Australia to the Maya civilization of southern Mexico. Good, informative reading.

4
The Archeological
Sequence in Texas

Most of the parks and museums described in this book feature interpretive centers where visitors may see artifacts from sites in the park and where there are dramatic dioramas, maps, and literature designed to describe and explain the archeology of the park. One aspect of interpretation is the placement of local archeology within the terms of what is known about the archeology of the state as a whole. That is done, in part, by identifying artifact collections as local representatives of archeological units called either periods or stages (Fig. 1).

The distinction between the terms is not particularly important here. Each refers to essentially the same kind of thing: an archeologically defined unit that corresponds roughly to a unique cultural pattern that existed at some time in the past. The idea these terms convey combines a collection of artifacts (thought to represent a particular culture, a particular way of life) with time.

The stages roughly correlate with the stages of sociocultural evolution discussed earlier. Dates for each stage are given in years before present (B.P.). Readers interested in detailed descriptions of artifacts are referred to the publications by Turner and Hester (1985), Suhm, Krieger, and Jelks (1954), and Suhm and Jelks (1962), listed at the end of this chapter, or many of the references listed at the end of each site description.

Paleoindian Stage (12,000–8,000 B.P.)

This stage represents the earliest known human populations in Texas, the hunters and gatherers who lived here when glacial ice covered much of the North American continent. In the present continental United States, a major glacial ice mass extended almost as far south as

St. Louis, while secondary glaciations were as far south as the mountains of southern New Mexico. Although there were no major direct effects of glacial ice in Texas, the climate here was greatly affected. The rainfall was greater, and the climate was milder. Correlated with those climatic differences, plant and animal life was considerably different, and Pleistocene megafauna such as mammoths, a giant species of buffalo, camels, saber-toothed tigers, and horses were common.

The term "Paleoindian" indicates that these people lived in the Ice Age and often hunted the large Ice Age animals. Both of the best-known, best-documented early human cultural complexes, the Clovis Complex and the Folsom Complex, have been identified at numerous sites throughout the southwestern United States and are well represented at sites in Texas.

The Clovis Complex (11,500–11,000 B.P.). In its simplest form, the Clovis Complex consists of three elements: *Clovis* points, associated mammoth remains, and numerous radiocarbon dates that cluster about 11,200 years ago. There are additional elements, but those three are the major characteristics of the complex. The people of the Clovis Complex have been called big-game hunters, since mammoth remains are so often associated with them. Recent interpretations have tended to downplay the big-game hunting aspect, however, and portray the people responsible for this complex as more typical hunters and gatherers who had the capability for taking large Pleistocene animals but were not dependent upon them.

Archeologists know little else about them. We do know that Clovis flintknappers were skilled craftsmen who made the quite distinctive *Clovis* fluted point. The *Clovis* point is easily recognized by its characteristic shape, ground basal edges, and, most of all, the large flake scars removed from the base on either side. It is generally conceded that those features facilitated hafting, or attaching, the projectile point to a shaft. *Clovis* points have been found in almost all parts of the New World, in Alaska and Canada and on the tip of South America as well as many points in between. Only in the southwestern United States, however, have *Clovis* points been found in close stratigraphic association with mammoth remains and charcoal samples adequate for radiocarbon testing. In this sense, the Clovis Complex has been identified only in the Southwest.

The origin of this complex is obscure. Logic suggests that earlier Clovis Complex sites should occur between the Southwest and Siberia, since the earliest human populations seem to have come to the New World by way of the Bering Strait area. Valid Clovis Complex sites have not yet been discovered except in the southwestern United States.

Figure 1. A Summary Guide to the Archeological Sequence in Texas

ARCHAIC

Period Years B.P.	Diagnostic Artifacts	Panhandle-Plains	Central Prairies	Pineywoods	Edwards Plateau/ Hill Country	South Texas	Trans-Pecos
Historic Proto-historic 450	European artifacts			Los Adaes	San Antonio missions	San Juan Bautista Padre Island	Fort Davis
Late Prehistoric 1,200	Pottery Points: *Perdiz*	Alibates		Caddoan Mounds			Hueco Tanks
Upper 3,000	*Scallorn* *Ensor* *Frio* *Bulverde*				McKinney Falls		
Middle Early 8,000	*Pedernales* *Tortugas* *Nolan* *Pandale*		Copper Breaks		Seminole Canyon	Falcon	
Paleoindian 12,000	*Plainview* *Folsom* *Clovis*	Caprock Canyon Lubbock Clovis	Lewisville		Aquarena Springs		

1. The archeological sequence in Texas. The sites described in this book are included in this chart. Only those archeological cultures featured in descriptions are presented.

The Clovis Site, described in this book, is the type site for the complex, because it was there, near Clovis, New Mexico, that the complex was first discovered during quarrying operations in the early thirties. Texas sites include the Lubbock Lake Site, Aquarena Springs, and the Lewisville Site.

The Folsom Complex (11,000–10,200 B.P.). The Folsom Complex, like the Clovis Complex, consists of three basic characteristics: *Folsom* points, associated fossil remains of Pleistocene bison, and consistent carbon dates to about 10,500 years ago. Although *Folsom* points are not as widespread as *Clovis* points, stratified Folsom Complex sites have been discovered from the northern Great Plains almost to the Gulf of Mexico.

Folsom flintknappers produced an artifact, the *Folsom* point, that has, by our standards at any rate, a jewellike quality. It is rather small and delicately crafted, and it has, similar to *Clovis* points, fluting scars. Unlike Clovis, however, the Folsom fluting technique generally consisted of the removal of one large flake from the base on either side of the point. The result is a dramatically thinned point with prominent fluting scars extending over most of the surface of both sides. Along with the finely chipped retouching of the cutting edge and the grinding of up to half of the lateral edges, *Folsom* points are a marvel of lithic technology. The aesthetic value of these artifacts seemed to be deliberately enhanced by their frequent manufacture from exotic stone; that is, *Folsom* points are often of stone not ordinarily found at a site but that was imported from some distance away. Volcanic glass was sometimes used, and Alibates flint was frequently used.

The people who produced the Folsom Complex lived during the end of the Ice Age glaciations and were the last we know of to hunt the large, Pleistocene buffalo. Since remains of these animals, along with radiocarbon dates consistently in the 10,200-year-old range, associated with *Folsom* points comprise the basic Folsom Complex, it is tempting to say that the Folsom peoples were direct descendents of the earlier Clovis peoples. That apparently straightforward conclusion is strengthened by radiocarbon dates indicating that the Folsom Complex is more recent than Clovis, and at sites such as Lubbock Lake and the Clovis Site where both complexes have been identified, Clovis is always stratigraphically lower than Folsom.

Although quite a lot of evidence suggests a direct relationship between the Clovis peoples and the Folsom peoples, none of the evidence is strong enough to merit that conclusion. There are, for example, no known transitional sites. Such a site would have elements of both complexes in association and thereby provide the necessary link between the two complexes that is currently missing. Folsom sites described in this book include the Clovis Site, Lubbock Lake, and the Lake Theo Site at Caprock Canyons State Park. The quarries at Alibates National Monument provided material for the Folsom toolmakers.

Other Paleoindian manifestations (10,200–8,000 B.P.). As the major glaciation of the most recent episode of the Ice Age retreated, the climate in Texas grew warmer and drier. With that change in climate, the Pleistocene megafauna so characteristic of the Ice Age gradually became extinct. During the period of transition, a number of late Paleoindian cultures replaced the Folsom Complex. The origin of these groups, their relationship, if any, to earlier groups, and what became of them are unknown.

The main things known about them involve the types of projectile points they left behind. Such types as *Plainview, Lerma, Golondrina, Angostura,* and *Firstview* have been found associated with the fossil remains of horses, the lingering remnants of typical Ice Age species in North America, as well as other more recent species such as modern buffalo (*Bison bison*). Of sites discussed in this book, late Paleoindian occupations have been reported at Lubbock Lake, Clovis, Aquarena Springs, Caprock Canyons, and Seminole Canyon. These sites are summarized in relation to others in Figure 1.

Archaic Stage (8,000 B.P.–Historic Contact)
The term "Archaic" is used here to indicate all post-

Pleistocene hunting and gathering cultures. The dates suggested above are inexact, but are intended to be. The period between the major climatic changes at the end of the Ice Age and the onset of the modern climate was marked by extreme fluctuations in local climates. Corresponding to climatic fluctuations, a tremendous variation in regional cultural adaptation seemed to develop. Upheaval in cultural expression seems to have been universally experienced wherever human populations were affected by the changing conditions. In Europe, for example, the post-Pleistocene variations are collectively known as the Mesolithic, and there, as here in Texas, there was a sudden proliferation of cultural forms and an overall growth of human populations.

The Archaic is by far the longest period of human occupation in Texas, so it is perhaps no wonder that examples of the Archaic culture have been discovered in all areas of Texas. Archaic sites—the most common type of prehistoric site in Texas—occur in practically every county in the state. At various times during the Archaic, areas that are now virtually unoccupied by humans were among the most heavily occupied regions of their day. At the opposite extreme, areas such as Houston and Dallas, with the largest modern populations, were unoccupied during the Archaic.

One general response to the climatic changes that occurred during the early phases of glacial retreat seemed to be the ever more intensive use of local resources. This conclusion is based on the observation that although few different types of artifacts of the Paleoindians are found at widely spaced sites over a large area, a variety of artifacts of the Archaic peoples are concentrated in distinct regional clusters. With a few exceptions (Aquarena Springs, for example), the people in Paleoindian cultures tended to be more nomadic than the Archaic peoples and had relatively few types of tools. They "skimmed the cream" from the food chain. The Archaic peoples, on the other hand, seemed to practice a more "tethered" style of nomadism; that is, they restricted their annual cyclic movements to a much smaller area than the Paleo hunters. At the same time, their larger tool kit allowed more facile use of the local environments. For example, seed-grinding tools such as manos and metates are characteristic of the Archaic but are almost unknown in Paleoindian assemblages.

Along with the increasing intensity of exploitation of the local environment and the corresponding diversity of tool types, there was a remarkable, but uneven, growth in population size and density in the Archaic. The human population in Texas at the close of the last Ice Age glaciation must have been very small. There are few late Paleoindian sites (though many more are known than either Clovis or Folsom sites), but thousands of Archaic sites are known in Texas. The proximity and length of habitation of the sites in some areas, such as Seminole Canyon, indicate a relatively large, dense, and sedentary population, a situation unknown in Texas during the Paleoindian occupation of the state.

Archaic populations are identified today on the basis of certain artifacts, stone artifacts for the most part, that have been considered diagnostic of the various societies and cultures that left them behind. For purposes of description, the lengthy and complex Archaic is often divided into arbitrary units such as the Early, Middle, and Late Archaic. For the sake of simplicity, such terms as "Transitional Archaic," "Neo Archaic," and other, similar terms used to refer to late prehistoric hunting and gathering occupations are here included in the Late Archaic. Each is identified on the basis of regional clusters of various types of artifacts, with an emphasis on projectile point types.

A summary of major artifact types considered diagnostic of Archaic cultures of the various regions in Texas is included in Figure 1. There are thousands of Archaic sites in Texas, but only sites described in this book are listed. Perhaps future books of this sort will be able to include more Archaic sites that are readily available for public visitation.

Late Prehistoric Stage
(ca. 1,200 B.P.–Historic Contact)

The uncertain dates for this stage accurately reflect the uncertain definition of its beginning and end, as is characteristic of historic (or prehistoric) processes. It often becomes necessary to draw arbitrary distinctions. Sometimes it seems unusually difficult to form a basis for even arbitrary distinctions. Such is the case in the Late Prehistoric.

The process of more and more intensive utilization of local environments continued throughout the Early and Middle Archaic, so that near the end of the Late Archaic many local populations began to have what was, for them, the high-tech tools of the day: bows and arrows and pottery. The groups were still, as far as we now know, hunters and gatherers, and therefore are classified as Archaic. Some of these Archaic peoples maintained a hunting and gathering subsistence until after historic contact.

Beginning about 1,200 years ago (A.D. 800), people began to produce food in the area that is now Texas. This innovation was not immediately and universally adopted. Consequently, many groups continued their hunting and gathering way of life until much more recent times. Those groups that adopted the techniques of plant domestication (principally corn and beans) are those classed as Late Prehistoric. (Sometimes "Neo-American," an older term, is used.) They were dominant in the Piney-woods, parts of the Panhandle-Plains, and the far western parts of the Trans-Pecos at the time of historic contact. The period of transition from hunting and gathering to food production remains a topic of particular concern in archeology. In Texas we have tremendous potential for the study of this transitional period. In South Texas there is the possibility that locally domesticated species will be found, and in East Texas there is an excellent opportunity to study the effect of the influx of food-producing peoples on local hunting and gathering populations.

Protohistoric Stage (No Date)

This stage is poorly defined and is perhaps more a concept than a particular stage. In one respect, the term "Protohistoric" refers to those cultures that are known about historically but without actual historic contact. For example, many documents in Spanish archives list groups of Indians by name. Typically the records are confusing to anyone attempting to make a historical connection between any of the names and a specifically known group. The names refer to protohistorically known groups. We know in a general historic sense about these groups, but we don't know where they were, who they were, or even if they actually were distinct entities. Sorting these protohistoric problems continues to be one of the premier problems in archeology worldwide, and Texas is no exception.

Another common kind of protohistoric group would be a group whose existence is known archeologically during historic times but for which there are no known historic records. Thus, in a narrow sense, the group would be a prehistoric group (no records, therefore no history), but since historic material was found associated with the remains of their culture, they are protohistoric. A good example of such a protohistoric group was explored by members of the Texas Archeological Society at the first of the annual TAS summer field schools, held in 1962 at the Gilbert Site (41RA13) in Rains County (Jelks 1967). In the course of investigations, a wealth of historic material was recovered. These artifacts of European manufacture included buttons and ornaments, kettles, gun parts (particularly gun flints), knives, chisels, beads and other trade items. Most of the items were identified as to approximate source and date of manufacture, and yet they were found in association with native American materials of unknown origin. The Gilbert Site thus provides an excellent example of a protohistoric site.

Historic Stage (Historic Contact–Present)

With the exception of the tenuously defined Protohistoric, the Historic Stage is contained in the shortest period of any of the stages in Texas archeology. The beginning of this stage varies according to the time of introduction of written records in a given area. Thus in one case, history can be said to begin in San Antonio early in the eighteenth century, when Spanish explorers and missionaries visited the site and maintained a written record of their visit. History in Dallas, however, began only in the mid-nineteenth century, about 150 years after history began in San Antonio.

Whenever it began and wherever it began, the Historic Stage marks a period of rapid cultural and social shifting in Texas, as elsewhere, and is the major topic of concern in historical archeology. Historical archeology is one of the fastest-growing areas of modern archeology in Texas, although in other areas it has long been the major area of archeological interest.

Classical archeology, which can be traced to early excavations at Pompeii and Herculaneum, is one of the earliest expressions of archeological interest. Classical archeology is a form of historical archeology. Archeology of this sort has long been a national passion in countries such as Italy, Greece, Israel, England, and France. Generally speaking, prehistoric archeology is a recent invention. In Texas, and in the New World in general, historical archeology has lagged behind the development of prehistoric archeology. That situation has been changing rapidly within the last few years, however, and historical archeology is now quite likely at least as large an area of specialization as prehistoric archeology. By the end of the century, historical archeology will probably be by far the most common practice of archeology in Texas.

References

These titles are helpful in getting an overview of Texas archeology. Some are out of date; some are the most current sources available. Some of them are very specific; others are quite general. All are recommended.

Hester, Thomas R., and Dee Ann Story (editors). In press. *The Archeology of Texas.* San Diego: Academic Press. Compiled by two of the most knowledgeable and respected professional archeologists in Texas, this long-awaited book is sure to remain the most complete and authoritative source about archeology in the state for many years to come.

Jelks, Edward B. (editor). 1967. The Gilbert Site: A Norteño Focus site in northeastern Texas. *Bulletin of the Texas Archeological Society* 37 (for 1966). The entire volume of this annual publication of the Texas Archeological Society is devoted to the report of the first summer field school sponsored by the society. The excavations at the Gilbert Site represent a milestone in growth of archeology in the state and provide a good example of an exercise in protohistorical archeology.

Suhm, Dee Ann, and Edward B. Jelks (editors). 1962. *Handbook of Texas Archeology: Type Descriptions.* Austin: Texas Archeological Society, Special Publication No. 1, and Texas Memorial Museum, Bulletin No. 4. This loose-leaf volume was intended as the first of a series of updates of the classic *Handbook of Texas Archeology,* with new descriptions to be added and old ones revised or discarded as needed. It didn't work out that way, however. Since pottery types as well as stone tools are included, it remains the best single source for descriptions of Texas prehistoric artifacts.

Suhm, Dee Ann, Alex D. Krieger, and Edward B. Jelks. 1954. *An Introductory Handbook of Texas Archeology.* Bulletin of the Texas Archeological Society, Vol. 25. This now classic summary of Texas archeology is, of course, now out of date in many respects. It has at the same time maintained a high degree of validity in concept and execution. If only one volume could be selected to understand Texas archeology, this would be the one. Unfortunately, although this effect was unintended, the handbook came to be used as the final word in Texas archeology rather than simply as the comprehensive summary it was intended to be. It was never republished or updated in new editions. Consequently, it is difficult to get a copy of this book. Highly recommended.

Turner, Ellen Sue, and Thomas R. Hester. 1985. *A Field*

Guide to Stone Artifacts of Texas Indians. Austin: Texas Monthly Press. This volume is an excellent source for illustration, description, dating, and affiliation of most of Texas' recognized stone tool types. Highly recommended for more detailed information concerning artifacts mentioned in this chapter.

5
The Nature of Archeological Sites

Sometimes it seems that archeologists forget that the way they use the word "site" is not always clearly understood. Sometimes it is misunderstood to mean roughly the same as "sight," in a tourist sense of "That's a sight to see!," or it is thought to refer only to spectacular ruins such as those at Mesa Verde in southern Colorado or Teotihuacán in Mexico. The term "site" also is often confused with what might better be called "locality." Since this book is primarily concerned with archeological sites, this section is intended as a discussion of the uses of the term.

Generally, the word "site" means the same thing in archeology as in everyday usage, in the sense of a specific location, a geographic place. It seems rather simple in this sense. So one can refer to a building site, a campsite, or a dedication site and have a feeling of comprehension. In a general sense, that is the way the word is intended in archeology.

One begins to encounter problems, however, when the word is specifically applied. For example, consider something as complex as a town. The term "townsite" is useful until one refers to a specific house within the town. Then, perhaps, we could consider the house site as a subdivision of the townsite, but what if the house represented by the house site was occupied several hundred years before the town represented by the townsite? This seems tedious, but it is the type of quandary archeologists regularly encounter when it is necessary to tailor the language to fit the needs of the discipline. In a situation similar to the one above, imagine an area along the banks of a creek where concentrations of burned rock, mussel shell, charcoal and ashes, and flint fragments are found dispersed over an area of several thousand square feet. Is this one site, several sites, or many sites?

Consider, for example, the human occupations that have been discovered in Yellowhouse Draw and that form an important part of the Lubbock Lake Landmark described later in this book. These occupations have variously been referred to as the Lubbock Lake Site, the Lubbock Lake Landmark, and the Lubbock Lake locality. Cultural materials found in this landmark represent some of the earliest evidence of human occupation in North America. Some of the finds at Lubbock Lake are recent, but many are representative of the earliest known occupations in Texas. Should this be called a site?

Such problems of terminology are mentioned here to prepare the reader for the ambiguity of archeological terms. The following discussion of certain archeological concepts is intended as a guide to the way terms are used in this book.

In archeology, the term "site" generally refers to a geographic location where evidence of human behavior has been noted. The evidence is usually in the form of durable artifacts such as stone tools, fences, burials, metal toys, or baskets. Behavior may be inferred from a worn pathway, the presence at an unexpected place of "natural" items whose transport is attributed to human activity, or simply collections from the natural environment made in such a way as to suggest human intervention. Thus, depending on criteria chosen more or less arbitrarily, archeologists have defined sites in various ways. Three major categories of sites found in Texas are occupational sites, special-purpose sites, and incidental sites.

Occupational Sites

This category includes all sites where people have lived for an extended period. The problem, of course, is what is to define "extended." Anywhere a person has been is a place where a person has lived. If a person just passes through an area and only momentarily stops to take a drink of water, this is obviously outside the meaning of "extended." What about a stay of several hours? A day?

The question is not easily resolved.

One could say that an occupational site is a place where resources are gathered. In this case a modern, temporary store-and-lock facility would constitute an occupational site. Although some store-and-lock facilities may actually represent places where people have lived for extended periods, that is not the intended use of such places. The point here is to reemphasize the ambiguous aspect of these definitions. Site types are meant to be useful but not mutually exclusive categories. Types of sites (as, indeed, all types of types) tend to overlap and emphasize characteristics that have proven to be utilitarian. Some types of occupational sites that may easily be visited in Texas are listed here.

Open campsites. This is the most common type of prehistoric site in Texas. Open campsites range in size from small overnight camps, occupied on only one occasion, to areas of several acres repeatedly occupied for extended periods. These sites are found in the open, usually near a reliable water source, and are marked by evidence of the use of fire, stone tools, debris and debitage of stone tool manufacture, shell, and ecofacts. Open camps may be seen at most sites described in this book, such as Caprock Canyons, Palo Duro Canyon, Seminole Canyon, Hueco Tanks, Lubbock Lake, Alibates, Copper Breaks, and Aquarena Springs.

Cave and rockshelter campsites. The interior of a cave rarely proves to be the site of human occupation. A cave interior might have been used for other purposes, but caves per se never have been popular places to live. The popular idea of "caveman" has little meaning in the sense of dwelling place. Spectacular sites such as Lascaux in southwestern France and Altamira in northern Spain are world-famous cave sites, but although they are distinguished by paintings in the interior, there is little evidence of occupation inside the cave. The occupation of such sites is almost always near the mouth.

In this sense cave and rockshelter camps are similar. Both are protected from the elements by overhanging rock. The difference is that rockshelters tend to be more open and have no dark, cramped interior. Rockshelters and areas at cave mouths are favored occupation sites wherever they are encountered. Easily visited rockshelter sites in Texas include those at Seminole Canyon, Hueco Tanks, and McKinney Falls.

Villages. Villages are distinguished from campsites by the nature of the architecture, the built environment. Villages have structures such as houses that require considerable effort to construct and are intended for lengthy habitation. In contrast to campsites, villages are also characterized by a relatively large population with high population density and increased complexity associated with social stratification.

There is no clear distinction between a large, relatively permanent campsite and a small village. Perhaps in an evolutionary sense the latter tends to develop from the former. Similarly, at the other extreme of village development, the distinction between a village and some larger, more complicated site such as a small city is often arbitrary. Prehistoric villages easily visited in Texas include Caddoan Mounds and Alibates Pueblo. Historic villages are associated with most of the historic localities, such as the San Antonio Missions, Guerrero, Los Adaes, and La Bahia.

Special-Purpose Sites

These are places where particular activities were undertaken. Sometimes the site has an obvious attraction that was a determining factor in the location of the activities. If, for example, people needed clay to make pottery, it would be necessary to get the clay. The location of the clay would determine the location of the activity of getting clay. The clay site would then be a special-purpose site. The Alibates flint quarries are excellent examples of special-purpose sites of this sort.

Another sort of special-purpose site is not so easily identified. The problem lies in determining the activities that were carried out. The activities may have represented a special purpose, but then maybe, from the point of view of the people who supposedly performed the activities, they could have been performed anywhere. At these sites the term "special purpose" is clearly of archeologists' choosing and may have nothing significant to say about the prehistoric activities at the site. An example of a special-purpose site of this sort would include a ceremonial center or other place where we infer that ceremonial behavior occurred. Certain aspects of rock art—either petroglyphs, as at the Alibates Pueblo, or pictographs, as at Panther Cave in Seminole Canyon—can be seen as involving ceremonial components. In this sense these sites could be considered as special-purpose sites, specifically, ceremonial centers. Similarly, but at a more complex level, the mounds at Caddoan Mounds certainly must have been involved in ceremonial behavior. In this sense, then, Caddoan Mounds can be considered a ceremonial site.

As pointed out earlier, these categories are somewhat arbitrary and tend to overlap. The Fate Bell Shelter contains deep, stratified occupational deposits and is a classic example of an occupied rockshelter site. Similarly, Caddoan Mounds represents much more than a ceremonial center. It is an excellent example of a Late Prehistoric, agricultural, settled farming village, probably the best example of this type of site in Texas. Yet it may have been founded as a ceremonial center. How should these sites be classified? That is the question.

The best rule of thumb in classification, whether in archeology or any other field, is the rule of convenience. Classes are best identified on the basis of distinctions considered important to the classifier. Sites are divided into types on the basis of ideas that archeologists think are important. The trick is to be aware of the ideas that underlie a given classification. It is necessary to understand the rules in order to play the game well.

Incidental Sites

As defined earlier, an archeological site is any geographic location where evidence of human behavior can be found. Usually the evidence indicates the activity was performed at a selected site, a place chosen for occupation, resource collection, some religious activity, and so on. Often, however, sites are found where the idea of selection cannot be justified.

Discovery of a single, isolated projectile point in an open field with no other known evidence within hundreds of feet could be incidental to the well-known arrow shot into the air that came down . . . where? In other words, the presence of the evidence at a specific place may be accidental, providential, an act of God, or, simply, incidental. The presence of artifacts at a particular place may have no relationship to the intentions of the people responsible for the artifacts. The Padre Island shipwrecks provide an excellent example of one kind of incidental site. No one could imagine that the Spanish ships would have been driven ashore at that location. The site of such an event then is correctly considered an incidental site. Subsequent sixteenth-century efforts by the Spanish to salvage material from the wrecks (or even more recent efforts by treasure hunters and the State of Texas) does not change the initial classification of the wrecks as incidental sites.

Often, potential archeological sites are identified before evidence of human behavior is found. These sites are identified on the basis of evidence that either has been associated with human behavior or can be expected to be associated with human behavior. For instance, no artifacts had been found at a site near Clovis, New Mexico, at the time that a mammoth tooth was uncovered there, but previous experience had established an association between such ecofacts and human behavior. The site was considered an incidental site until subsequent discoveries established it to be an open campsite.

Renewable and Nonrenewable Sites

As an interesting afterthought, consider this. Archeological sites in Texas are endangered. There is no question that evidence of previous human behavior is vanishing. Furthermore, loss of this evidence is regrettable in the same sense that growing old is regrettable:

it seems to be the natural order of things. We cannot preserve all archeological sites for some of the time or even some sites all the time, but we can, and should, preserve some of them some of the time.

It has been said that archeological sites are nonrenewable resources. Certainly, that is true, but only in a narrow and trivial sense. In the same sense each breath we take is a nonrenewable resource, and evidence of any event is nonrenewable. In fact, archeological sites are as renewable as anything else. At Padre Island, the wreckage of the Spanish ships surely will not be repeated again. The site is nonrenewable. But artifacts left behind by the people involved in the various salvage operations have in turn created sites that no doubt include occupational, special-purpose, and incidental types. Archeological sites can be considered perpetually renewable—at least as long as there are human beings, and then perhaps it won't matter anymore.

The important question is not whether an archeological site, or any evidence of the past, is renewable or nonrenewable. The real question is what we will make of these resources. We can destroy them in a willful and ignorant way, as so many have been destroyed in the past, or we can continue to build and improve the type of program of selection and presentation illustrated by the sites described in this volume.

The Idea of Prehistory

Up to this point, types of archeological sites have been distinguished on the basis of functional criteria. Thus there are places where people lived (occupational sites), places where particular activities were performed (special-purpose sites), and places where function cannot be readily attributed (incidental sites). But it is possible to use any of a number of greatly differing criteria to distinguish various types of sites and thereby attain an entirely different outlook. Consider, for example, the common, basic distinction between historic and prehistoric sites. The distinction first depends on whether there is a history of the site, "history" here meaning a known, extant, written record. This concept of history then invites the concept of what preceded history.

Generally speaking, there is one concept of time that dominates thought in Western Civilization. This concept is so ingrained, so pervasive, that Westerners take it as given, a fact. It is so much a part of our cultural heritage that we cannot imagine a world without time—our kind of time.

Our concept of time is expressed metaphorically in a number of ways. For example, "Time is like a river, a river of no return." We think of time as a one-directional sequence of events, from the past, through the present, to the future. In keeping with this concept of time, we have developed methods, techniques, and rituals for developing adequate accounts of events. Some of the rules for developing such accounts are discussed in Chapter 2, Archeology. Here we are concerned with the typical presentation of these accounts at publicly accessible archeological sites in Texas.

When we think of the past, we think of those events that have happened as well as the sequence of their happening. On a personal basis, this could be called memory. After several generations no one alive can remember the events, and the account of them begins to take on more obviously mythical properties. If writing is available, such accounts are often written. This is basic history—a written account of past events. If writing is not available, or if the written accounts are lost or cannot be translated, neither memory nor history are adequate to express the events and the sequence that our concept of time demands. We know things happened but not just what happened or when.

The time before history begins in a particular area is known as prehistory. That simple idea has some difficult implications associated with it. For example, Texas is a new area historically, since our earliest historical accounts go back no farther than the accounts of European adventurers. The earliest histories, as such, are even more recent. Structures such as an early twentieth-century home in the Texas Panhandle are of particular interest to historic archeologists in an area such as Texas, where there is a very attenuated history. The histories of even our oldest cities, such as El Paso, Nacogdoches, or San Antonio, extend no farther into the past than the early eighteenth century. Histories of our newer cities, such as Dallas and Houston, date only from the mid-nineteenth century, and the history of most of the rest of the state is even more recent. Even within Texas, it is obvious that parts of the state are historically known for a period in which other areas have no history and therefore are prehistoric.

Thus, a common classification of sites depends on whether they are historic or prehistoric. In the discussion of periods of cultural development in Texas, for example, the most recent period is often listed as the Historic Period. It is somewhat confusing, since other types of criteria are used to distinguish earlier periods. It is important to consider the categories into which we sort archeological sites, because the categories define our treatment of the sites as well as our understanding of the people whose actions we see as responsible for them.

Further Reading

The idea of archeological sites is discussed in several easily obtained sources; the following are among them.

Hester, Thomas R., Robert F. Heizer, and John A. Graham. 1975. *Field Methods in Archaeology,* 6th edition. Palo Alto, California: Mayfield. This edition of the classic field manual presents excellent discussions of sites as sites and gives many examples of various sites in Texas as well as the rest of the world. Highly recommended.

Joukowsky, Martha. 1980. *A Complete Manual of Field Archaeology: Tools and Techniques of Field Work for Archaeologists.* Englewood Cliffs, New Jersey: Prentice-Hall. Although the portion of this book dedicated to

explicit discussion of sites as sites is a relatively in-
significant part of the whole, the concept of site perme-
ates all sections. This is a useful book in many regards,
and the feeling one gets about the nature of archeological sites is an important quality conveyed in its
pages.

Vita-Finzi, C. 1978. *Archaeological Sites in Their Setting*.
London: Thames and Hudson. This book is one of the
best statements available concerning sites as sites.
It is direct in approach, clear in meaning. Unfortunately,
it is not easily obtained.

6
Guide to Archeological Sites in Texas

The following site descriptions are presented in groups that correspond to natural geographic variations in Texas. This practice is customary for two reasons. First, it is a convenient way to group sites in a general guide. All the sites in an area can be lumped together and presented as a unit. In a state as large as Texas, that is useful in a variety of ways.

When cultural material is grouped by geographic proximity, an interesting pattern often emerges. It would be safe to say that cultural items from the same area tend to be similar in comparison to items from farther away. Yet, sometimes relatively nearby cultural traits are very different, indicating that distance is not the only factor involved. Other important factors include topography, climate, soils, and types of plants and animals. All those features are included in the concept of natural regions.

The idea has long been used by anthropologists and cultural geographers to plot cultural variations and explain them, in part, by reference to geographical factors. For archeologists, the idea has a time dimension with interesting variations. Not only is it possible to point out geographic variation in contemporaneous cultures, but it is also possible to study change through time as well as space. This idea formed one of the organizing principles of the influential *Introductory Handbook of Texas Archeology* (Suhm, Krieger, and Jelks 1954), and remains an important factor in archeological description and analysis.

Six major archeological and natural areas are identified here (Fig. 2). Further information about each area is included as appropriate within the context of individual site descriptions. Note that the sites chosen to be included are not equally distributed among the various natural areas. In a limited sense, the imbalance represents distortions of convenience, money, political power, and a host of other factors that have influenced many decisions far beyond the scope of this book. It is important to note, however, that the unequal distribution of sites through space and through time is an accurate indicator of important cultural changes in the past. The six regions are: Panhandle-Plains, Central Prairies, Pineywoods, Edwards Plateau/Hill Country, Southern Plains, and Trans-Pecos.

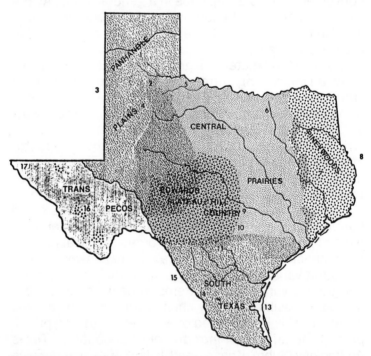

2. Natural and cultural areas of Texas. 1. Alibates Quarries. 2. Caprock Canyons. 3. Clovis. 4. Lubbock Lake. 5. Copper Breaks. 6. Lewisville. 7. Caddoan Mounds. 8. Los Adaes. 9. McKinney Falls. 10. Aquarena Springs. 11. San Antonio Missions. 12. Seminole Canyon. 13. Padre Island. 14. Falcon Lake. 15. San Juan Bautista. 16. Fort Davis. 17. Hueco Tanks.

Format of Site Descriptions

Site descriptions in this section are arranged in a standard format, providing a quick reference to salient features at each site. Many of the terms and concepts used here are explained earlier in this book, and the reader is referred to those chapters for more information. The descriptions are intentionally brief and selective and are intended to supply information about each site not easily available elsewhere. Elaborations on the standard interpretations are avoided, as they are usually available elsewhere. Readers who want more information concerning a particular site are encouraged to write or call personnel at the site or consult the publications listed at the end of each section.

Site name and address: This information was current at the time of final editing and in most cases will likely be correct for years to come.

General description: The purpose of this category is to specify the location of the site, along with directions on how to get to it, and to point out other information useful to visitors. Also included is information about the climate that might be helpful in planning a trip to the site.

Standard archeological interpretation: This category outlines the conventional thought about the site. Although the outlines are extreme simplifications, each is useful as an index of key terms and interpretations associated with the site. Since archeological sites are complex, the interpretations presented here should be seen as selective, not comprehensive. Those concepts and terms chosen as relevant at each site are emphasized.

Site: Sometimes the site name indicated here is the same as the official name listed above. Often, however, the official name is too general and covers several specific sites. The designation here refers more specifically to particular sites. For example, "Seminole Canyon State Historical Park" is the official name of one entry, but the Fate Bell Shelter and Panther Cave are specific sites referred to in that description.

Type of site: A general classification of the site according to its most characteristic features.

Developmental stage: A significant period of social and cultural evolution represented at the site.

Archeological period: The time frame assigned to the part of the site emphasized here.

Dates: If available, these refer to the specific time of the occupation or use of the site emphasized here.

Archeological culture: These names have been used for cultural materials at the site and are found in the archeological record.

Diagnostic traits: For quick reference, several of the most easily identified, characteristic types of artifacts associated with the sites are listed here. For further descriptions of traits, the reader should consult one of several typological handbooks, such as those by Suhm, Krieger, and Jelks (1954); Suhm and Jelks (1962); or Turner and Hester (1985). Many of the artifacts listed here are featured in displays at interpretive centers of the various sites and museums.

Comment: This part of the description is subjective and impressionistic. It is intended to convey some of the salient characteristics of the site that a visitor might expect to encounter.

Environment: The topography, geology, climate, plant and animal communities, and other environmental features are described in this section. The major objective is to emphasize the environment at each site. Environmental features were selected to characterize the site and are not intended to be comprehensive. The relationship between human beings and the specific geographic location can best be understood by visiting and studying the site in place. It is one aspect of human physical existence that cannot be moved to a museum.

Archeology: Selected aspects of the archeology of each site are featured in this category. Traditional interpretations are avoided, as they can be found in the interpretive center at many of these places. Some standard interpretation is included for those sites without interpretive centers. Readers are encouraged to pursue further information in the publications listed at the end of each section.

Further Reading

These publications were selected because most can be found in bookstores and libraries and do not require access to special or confidential information. The few exceptions are sources of quotations and other references necessary to emphasize a point. The lists throughout this chapter are suggestive and are not intended to be either comprehensive or definitive. Many of the sources cited include detailed lists of references, and the interested reader is referred to them.

Kingston, Mike (editor). 1987. *Texas Almanac 1988–1989*. Dallas: Dallas Morning News. Everyone in Texas should know and use the *Texas Almanac*. It is the handiest source of information about the state. In addition to the usual section on the environment of the state and other standards, it now regularly features matters of archeological interest. The almanac was the source of much of the environmental information in this book. Highly recommended.

Kroeber, A. L. 1963. *Cultural and Natural Areas of Native North America*. Berkeley: University of California Press. Originally published in 1939, this volume is a classic treatment on the theme of environmental relationships of Native American cultures in terms of distinct geographic units. It is very helpful in understanding Texas archeology in a broader perspective.

Suhm, Dee Ann, and Edward B. Jelks. 1962. *Handbook of Texas Archeology: Type Descriptions*. Austin: Texas Archeological Society, Special Publication No. 1, and Texas Memorial Museum, Bulletin No. 4. This looseleaf typological manual remains the best single source for identification of Texas artifact types. It features written and photographic descriptions of pottery as well as projectile point types.

Suhm, Dee Ann, Alex D. Krieger, and Edward B. Jelks.

1954. *An Introductory Handbook of Texas Archeology.* Bulletin of the Texas Archeological Society, Vol. 25. The classic typological manual of Texas archeology, this book is a collector's item itself. Recommended, but very hard to find.

Turner, Ellen Sue, and Thomas R. Hester. 1985. *A Field Guide to Stone Artifacts of Texas Indians.* Austin: Texas Monthly Press. This is a worthy continuation of the typological standardization of Texas artifacts. Very useful, it allows quick identification of diagnostic types. Highly recommended.

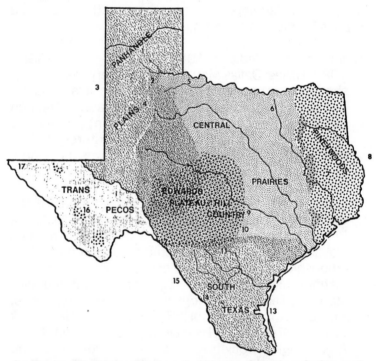

3. Panhandle-Plains Region. 1. Alibates Quarries. 2. Caprock Canyons. 3. Clovis. 4. Lubbock Lake. 5. Copper Breaks.

PANHANDLE-PLAINS REGION

The Texas Panhandle region is a southern extension of the Great Plains of North America. The most distinctive geographic feature of this part of the Southern Plains is a massive erosional remnant known as the Llano Estacado, or Staked Plains (Fig. 3). The Llano is defined on the north by the breaks of the Canadian River and by the Caprock on the eastern and western flanks. The southern boundary is not clearly marked but gradually blends into the Edwards Plateau.

Four important archeological sites—the Alibates flint quarries, the Lake Theo Folsom Site (Caprock Canyons), the Clovis Site, and the Lubbock Lake Site—are closely associated with the Llano and its ancient environment. Near the end of the last major glaciation, this was the most heavily populated part of Texas. Even so, there probably were fewer than 1,000 people living on the Llano. These four sites offer some of the best information available about them and the way they lived.

Alibates Flint Quarries and Texas Panhandle Pueblo Culture National Monument
P.O. Box 1438
Fritch, Texas 79036
(806) 857-3151

General description: The monument is about 30 miles north of Amarillo, Potter County, and 7.5 miles south-west of Fritch, Hutchinson County. To get there, turn west onto the clearly marked Alibates Road from Texas High-way 136 between Fritch and Amarillo at a point about 7.5 miles south of Fritch. From the turnoff it is about 6 miles to the Information Station at the monument en-trance. Current information can also be obtained at the National Park Service headquarters in Fritch. Alibates Na-tional Monument is operated by the National Park Ser-vice and is locally administered as a portion of the Lake Meredith National Recreation Area. It may be visited only during tours guided by park rangers. The tours are free and are scheduled daily at 10 A.M. and 2 P.M. from Memorial Day through Labor Day. Special tours may be scheduled by writing the superintendent at least five days in advance.
  Altitude: 3,600 feet above mean sea level
  Average annual precipitation: 20 inches
  Average January minimum temperature: 24°F
  Average July maximum temperature: 92°F

Standard archeological interpretation:
  Site: Alibates Quarries
  Type of site: Special-purpose
  Developmental stage: All stages
  Archeological period: All periods
  Dates: Since 12,000 years ago
  Archeological culture: Several
  Diagnostic traits: Quarries, lithic reduction debris and debitage

Site: Alibates Ruin
Type of site: Village
Developmental stage: Agriculture
Archeological period: Late Prehistoric
Dates: A.D. 1300–1450
Archeological culture: Antelope Creek Focus
Diagnostic traits: Ruins of masonry structures, stone tools such as *Harrell* and *Fresno* projectile point types and diamond-shaped beveled knives made from Alibates flint, hoe blades of bison scapulae, local pottery (*Borger* cordmarked), Puebloan pottery (*St. Johns* polychrome and *Lincoln* black-on-red)

Comment: With the construction of Sanford Dam in the early sixties, the U.S. Bureau of Reclamation created one of the few large lakes on the southern High Plains. Before impounded waters covered the area, salvage archeology was carried out and the entire area surveyed. Of the various archeological components that have been identified, two of the most significant are represented within this monument. One, the Alibates flint quarries, is arguably one of the most important prehistoric sites in the western hemisphere. Flint from this locality has been found in sites ranging in age from the earliest known human occupation of North America to historic times. Flint tools of Alibates origin have been identified at widely distributed sites in North America, from the Mississippi River basin to central Mexico. In addition to the flint quarries, the Alibates Creek Site provides an excellent example of a mixed Pueblo-Plains culture with fine masonry architecture and impressive petroglyphs.

Advisory: Don't visit Alibates expecting to see spectacular ruins or reconstructions. The locality is important from an archeological-anthropological perspective, but it is not for the lazy visitor.

Environment: Lake Meredith occupies part of the valley of the Canadian River. The headwaters of the Canadian lie in the eastern slopes of the Sangre de Cristo Mountains of northeastern New Mexico 200 miles to the west. From this point the river flows in a generally eastward direction until it joins the Arkansas River west of Fort Smith, Arkansas. The Canadian valley thus separates the Llano Estacado from the rest of the High Plains and provides an important, well-watered avenue of communication across the arid plains. (For a description of the Llano Estacado, see the Lubbock Lake Landmark section.) The Alibates National Monument lies along the mideastern portion of the Lake Meredith uplands, in the Canadian River "breaks," a term applied by topographers to an area significantly affected by stream erosion. The Canadian River breaks are an especially good example of that kind of topography. The area is well within the shortgrass prairie, the most arid of our midcontinent grasslands, and the general environment reflects this dryness. For contrast, plants characteristic of the mixed prairie are found at the Lubbock Lake Landmark only 150 miles to the south, and 200 miles to the west pine forests are characteristic of the Sangre de Cristo range. Three distinct microenvironments can be found at Alibates: the relatively flat uplands, the Canadian breaks, and a riverine zone.

Plants. The upland prairie is distinguished by blue grama (*Bouteloua gracilis*) and buffalo grass (*Buchloë dactyloides*), both nutritious forage grasses. The latter apparently existed in adaptive symbiosis with the American bison, hence the name.

Mesquite brush (*Prosopis glandulosa*) is today quite prominent throughout the Canadian breaks, although it is historically recent. Other trees and shrubs in the breaks include an occasional juniper (*Juniperus virginiana*) and post oak (*Quercus stellata*). Grasses include three-awn (*Aristida* spp.), bluestem (*Andropogon spp.*), and relict patches of tobosa (*Hilaria mutica*).

Throughout the southern High Plains the riverine zones are most often the locale for the largest trees. The willow (*Salix* spp.), cottonwood (*Populus deltoides*), and Mexican plum (*Prunus mexicana*) are characteristic along this part of the Canadian.

Animals. Until the late nineteenth century the dominant animal in this area was undoubtedly the buffalo (*Bison bison*). Pronghorn antelope (*Antilocapra americana*) once also populated the area in large numbers but are seldom seen today. The jackrabbit (*Lepus californicus*) and prairie dog (*Cynomys ludovicianus*) are the animals most commonly seen in the uplands today.

The Canadian breaks zone is characterized by striped skunks (*Mephitis mephitis*), cottontail rabbits (*Sylvilagus* spp.), and white-tailed deer (*Odocoileus virginianus*). Today, the riverine zone has such water-loving animals as the raccoon (*Procyon lotor*) and muskrat (*Ondatra zibethicas*). Overall, 59 species of mammals and more than 100 species of birds have been reported.

Archeology: Two significant aspects of the archeology at this park are represented by the Alibates quarries and the remains of the Pueblo-Plains villages found here.

Alibates Quarries

Approximately 1,000 shallow, open-pit flint quarries have been located within the present park boundaries. The quarries have been a source of raw material for chipped stone tools for more than 12,000 years. Some Alibates flint is quite distinctive and has been identified in association with mammoth remains at other sites in the Southwest; those sites are generally considered to be associated with the Clovis culture dated about 12,000 years ago. Alibates flint is also regularly found at Folsom sites that date to about 10,000 years ago. Unfortunately, there is no clear evidence of those early cultures within the Alibates area that can be directly related to quarrying activities.

The most significant feature of the quarries may be the clear evidence of stone tool manufacture. Following is a brief description of some fundamentals in the manufacture of chipped stone tools. The park rangers are most knowledgeable about stone tool manufacture, and they are helpful and eager to share their knowledge with visitors by giving demonstrations of tool making. With a little advance preparation, this can be the highlight of a trip to the Alibates quarries.

Primer in Basic Lithic Technology

The study of stone tools represents one of the most direct means of access we have to the psychology of prehistoric peoples. In that sense studying lithic technology is like peering into the mists of time to see ancient technologists at work. Because so much of the evidence of prehistoric peoples in Texas is in the form of stone artifacts, an understanding of the manufacturing process of chipped stone tools is important in the interpretation of the archeological record. The following summary is intended as an orientation to the process of lithic technology—the making of chipped stone tools.

The manufacture of chipped stone tools is a form of sculpture, a process of reduction in which a relatively large piece of stone is systematically reduced to approximate a desired shape and size. It is, in a modest sense, similar to the problem Michelangelo confronted each time he attempted the perfect rendition of a pietà, the Holy Mother, Mary, grieving over the body of Jesus after the Crucifixion. It is a problem all sculptors of stone must face: how to free a concept from the stone in which it is embedded.

The reconstruction of the process of reduction gives a glimpse of the thought processes, motor skills, and aesthetic preferences of the makers of the objects. A reconstruction is feasible, in part at least, because stone provides a relatively long-lasting record and because the reduction is a relatively simple and straightforward logical process—there aren't many different ways to make a chipped stone tool.

The two basic reduction techniques (variously known as chipping, flaking, or knapping techniques) use percussion or pressure to remove flakes from the stone. In the first, percussion flaking, the toolmaker strikes the flint (or other appropriate material) with another object. If the object is relatively hard stone (quartzite, for example), the resultant flake and flake scar are distinctive in shape. This is called hard hammer percussion, and the hammer is called a hammerstone.

If the object used to strike the flint is relatively soft (such as deer or elk antler), the flake as well as the resultant flake scar will have distinctive shapes quite different from those indicative of hard hammer percussion. The technique is known as soft hammer percussion flaking, and sometimes an antler hammer is referred to as a baton. One of the simple pleasures of elementary flint-knapping is to learn to recognize flakes of this sort. They are sometimes called "biface thinning flakes" because the technique is often used to thin bifacially chipped artifacts. Sometimes the flakes are simply referred to as "lipped flakes," since they are characterized by a noticeable ridge, or lip. If asked, the park rangers will probably be happy to demonstrate the techniques.

Once a student of archeology understands the basics of lithic reduction, he can approach archeology from a new, more promising perspective. Without knowledge of the manufacturing process, students usually focus on the end product, the tool. With knowledge of the process of reduction, they can determine much more about human behavior than was previously possible. Attention is no longer concentrated on end products but also on other artifacts, such as the refuse created as a by-product of that process (debris) and the pieces of material that may be further modified (debitage).

Besides technological features of culture such as motor skills, kinds of tools, and methods of application, other aspects of cultural behavior that may be determined from the analysis of chipped stone tools include psychological processes such as motivation and aesthetic value. For example, assuming the manufacture of stone tools was important, one measure of the degree of importance

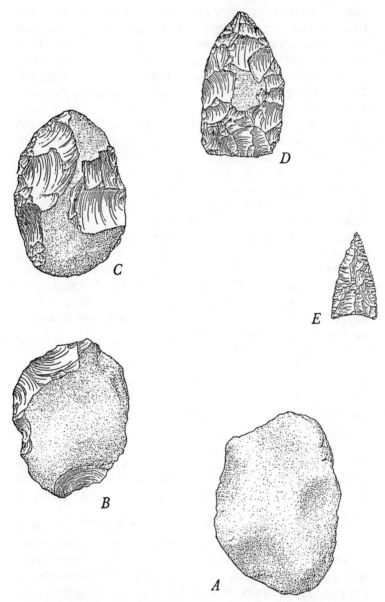

4. Sequence of stages in biface reduction. Beginning with a relatively large piece (A), the stone is systematically reduced in size and shape until the ideal form is approximated (E).

placed on the activity would be the amount of effort required to obtain the material used. This park affords an excellent example of that principle.

Alibates flint is easy to obtain here, and tools made of the material and used here would indicate no special motivation to use it. However, since this material occurs only here, tools of Alibates flint found at other sites can be used to measure the degree of motivation to use the flint at those locations. Flint from Alibates quarries found at sites hundreds of miles away is interpreted as evidence of strong psychological motivation in obtaining this material. It must have been important to the people who used it, and it must have been important to various groups of people for thousands of years. It is still important to us today.

Although the manufacturing process is relatively simple, it isn't necessarily easy. It requires not only the mental template that guides the toolmaker's progress but also skill and experience; a great deal of hand-eye coordination is necessary to produce satisfactory results. Figure 4 illustrates five steps in the production of a triangular biface, also often known as a projectile point, dart point, or arrowhead. **Stage A.** The initial stage of reduction is perhaps the most important. The material has been selected and tested, and flaked on one side. The side shown is prepared for reduction. **Stage B.** Reduction of this side commences with hard hammer percussion as indicated by characteristic flake scars. **Stage C.** Reduction continues with soft hammer as indicated by the distinctive long, relatively narrow flake scars. Shaping begins. **Stage D.** Shaping and thinning continue with soft hammer blows. **Stage E.** Final shaping and edge finish with pressure flaking.

Pueblo-Plains Villages

The largest of the village sites in the park area was formerly known as Alibates Ruin or simply Alibates 28 or A-45. This site represents one of the largest villages in the archeological culture known as the Antelope Creek

Focus of the Panhandle Aspect.

Alibates Ruin was almost obliterated by WPA crews in the late thirties and early forties. Figure 5 represents some of the more than fifty rooms that, along with a large number of pits of various sizes and depths, were exposed in the course of a complete excavation. In addition, numerous artifacts were recovered, and the work was

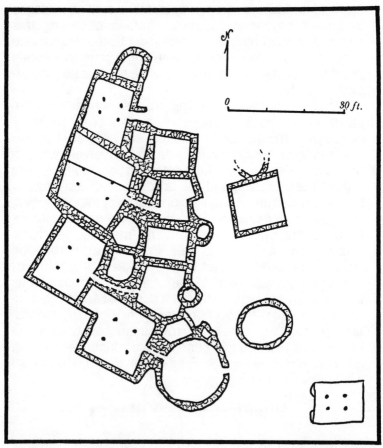

5. Structures at Alibates Village. This map was derived from field maps made by the WPA. Stone walls are indicated by mottled areas. Dots are postmolds.

documented with field notes, maps, and catalogs. This site stands as a monument to ill-conceived technique and purpose. All in all the "excavation" of the Alibates Ruin was more a semicontrolled destruction of a site than a meticulous, well-controlled, and recorded excavation.

For many years it was believed that the various ruins called the Antelope Creek Focus somehow represented people who were ancestors of the Puebloan cultures of New Mexico and other areas of the Southwest. Then, with the discovery of late Puebloan trade pottery associated with the villages of the Antelope Creek Focus, it was suggested that these peoples may have originated on the plains long after the Puebloan tradition had been started. It has also been suggested that the Panhandle Aspect peoples derived from earlier cultures in the Upper Republican River area of western Nebraska and the Chaquaqua Plateau of southeastern Colorado. The question of the origin of the people who built these structures remains open.

The people who built at Alibates did so in a 200-year period from about A.D. 1250 to 1450. They lived in generally contiguous multiroomed pueblos of up to 100 rooms. Rooms are rectangular, sometimes interconnected, and have tunneled entrances. The relatively infrequent, large, circular structures were probably ceremonial kivas. Construction employed rows of limestone (dolomite) slabs for a foundation and lower wall with adobe superstructure.

The people had a mixed economy, depending about equally on hunting and gathering and domesticated corn, beans, and squash. Evidence of wild species recovered during excavation includes animals such as buffalo, antelope, deer, turkey, and skunk. Wild plants are represented by acorns, cattail reeds, wild plum, and persimmon. Evidence suggests people in various settlements were exchanging food as well as trading for objects such as pottery, seashells, obsidian, and turquoise from more distant sources.

Shallow depressions in the shape of a human outline, two turtles, numerous shallow mortars, and two human tracks pecked into the surface of bedrock and boulders represent the most distinctive and memorable artifact type to be found at the Alibates Creek Site. The creators of these shallow depressions, a form of petroglyph, were almost surely associated with the Panhandle Aspect peoples, but this has not been clearly established. Although there are only a few petroglyphs to be seen at Alibates, they present an opportunity for interpretation not afforded by the technology of stone tool manufacture or architecture.

The original meaning of the representations is not understood in terms of modern archeology but can be understood in other ways. The human footprints, pecked in the dolomite bedrock at the rim of a small canyon overlooking a wide expanse of the surrounding plains and Canadian breaks, mark a significant point at the site where the past seems to flow into the present.

Further Reading

The following contain descriptions of the technique of chipped stone manufacture and more information about the Alibates Park area.

Turner, Ellen Sue, and Thomas R. Hester. 1985. *A Field Guide to Stone Artifacts of Texas Indians.* Austin: Texas Monthly Press. This book is a useful introduction to lithic tool technology with an emphasis on the manufacture of chipped stone tools and prehistoric projectile points in Texas. It includes outline drawings, descriptions, and dates of many projectile point types. Highly recommended.

Lowry, Jack, and Mike Lacey. 1988. "Alibates." *Texas Highways,* April, 1988:42–46. This well-illustrated article is informative about the Alibates site and about the type of instruction the rangers provide. Recommended.

Caprock Canyons State Park
P.O. Box 204
Quitaque, Texas 79255
(806) 455-1492

General description: To reach this park in the Texas Panhandle northeast of Lubbock, take Ranch Road 1065 for 3.5 miles north of Quitaque, Briscoe County. Acquired by the State in 1975, this huge park consists of almost 14,000 acres of rugged semidesert at the edge of the Caprock. There are 14 miles of trails and nature paths and an excellent small interpretive shelter displaying the ritual offering of bones from the Lake Theo Site (Fig. 6). Open daily May through August, from 8 A.M. to 9 P.M., and September through April, from 8 A.M. to 5 P.M. Standard state park admission fee.
   Altitude: 2,100–3,200 feet above mean sea level
   Average annual precipitation: 20 inches
   Average January minimum temperature: 26°F
   Average July maximum temperature: 94°F

Standard archeological interpretation:
   Site: Lake Theo Site
   Type of site: Open camp, special-purpose (butchering station)
   Developmental stage: Hunting and gathering
   Archeological period: Paleoindian
   Dates: More than 10,000 B.P. (Before Present)
   Archeological culture: Folsom Complex
   Diagnostic traits: *Folsom* points, *Bison antiquus*

Comment: For a variety of reasons this park is one of those in Texas most untouched by modern civilization. When nearby Mackenzie Reservoir was surveyed by archeologists, newspapers ran stories emphasizing the remoteness of the area as indicated by "tame" deer, quail, and snakes and remarking upon the general lack of pollution. The park is beautiful, and a visitor can, quite literally, get lost in it.

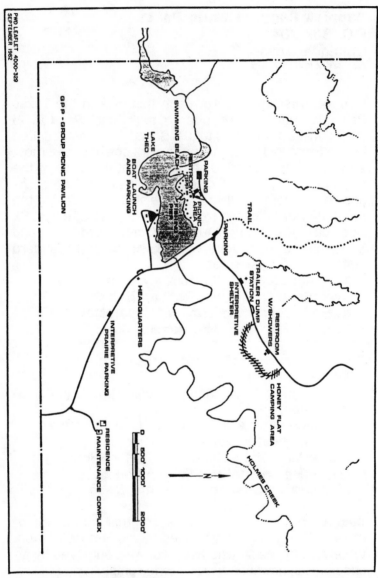

6. Caprock Canyons State Park. (Map courtesy Texas Parks and Wildlife Department.)

Environment: Located at the western edge of the rolling prairies, the park features rugged terrain that has been described as bad lands, or breaks, formed by erosion into underlying geologic formations. The western edge of the park is the most rugged, because it has the most recent cuts into the caprock formation. As one travels to the east, away from the Caprock, the terrain becomes smoother, and the term "rolling prairie" seems appropriately descriptive.

Geologic stratigraphy is impressive in the park area. The dominant redbed exposures are remains of a period geologists call the Permian. Between 225 million and 280 million years ago, the area was covered by a shallow sea; the reddish layers visible now are composed of siltstones and sandstones deposited at that time. During the next geologic period, known as the Triassic, 190 million to 225 million years ago, the area was uplifted, and streams eroded portions of earlier formations and redeposited them as light-brown sandstones and reddish or maroon shales visible in the park. The Tecovas formation is the source of jasper and other materials used in lithic tool manufacture. The major component visible in the caprock escarpment that forms the western cliffs at park headquarters is called the Ogallala formation. This formation, 200 to 600 feet thick, is characterized by gravels and silts washed down from the Rockies during the last of the Pliocene Epoch, 12 million to 2 million years ago. A thick caliche deposit forms the "cap" of the caprock; it is relatively hard and erosion resistant and is seen as the whitish cliffs along the edge of the caprock.

The dam forming Lake Theo was constructed across Holmes Creek, a local tributary of the Little Red River. The stream and others in the area drain much of the northern portion of the eastern Caprock escarpment and join the Prairie Dog Town Fork of the Red River several miles east of the park. Those streams form their erosional headcuts at the lowest points on the surface of the caprock. Away from the edge the low points form shallow lakes after rains. During extended rains, they fill up and flow into one another, thus forming a stream from one shallow point to another. The point where such a stream reaches the edge of the caprock is marked by a headcut of a stream similar to Holmes Creek and others in the park.

During the Pleistocene, rainfall in the area was much greater than in the present, and the streams flowed regularly. People lived along the streams and lakes, and the evidence of their presence was subsequently covered by alluvial and other deposits. Sometimes, deposits are removed by wind erosion, as in the vicinity of the Clovis Site (Blackwater Draw), or removed by dredging or other activity, as at Lubbock Lake, and the evidence is exposed once again. One especially interesting type of exposure occurs along the edge of the caprock at those points where headcuts breach the shallow ponds. An excellent example of such potentially valuable sites is on Holmes Creek upstream from Lake Theo.

Plants. Probably because of the rugged terrain, the park area provides some of the most varied wildlife habitats in the Texas Panhandle. It is a mixed-grass prairie dominated by buffalo grass (*Buchloë dactyloides*), blue grama (*Bouteloua gracilis*), and little bluestem (*Schizachyrium scoparium*). Prickly pear cactus (*Opuntia polyacantha*) and yucca (*Yucca glauca*) are found scattered throughout the park. Juniper (*Juniperus* spp.) and mesquite (*Prosopis glandulosa*) are dominant trees in upland and slope areas, and cottonwood (*Populus sargentii*), hackberry (*Celtis* spp.), and oak (*Quercus* spp.) are found where there is enough water.

Animals. The park is especially attractive for bird-watching. More than 175 species have been sighted, and the size and remote location of the park ensure optimal conditions. The area is especially attractive to migratory and resident waterfowl. Common sightings include mourning dove (*Zenaidura macroura*), bobwhite quail (*Colinus virginianus*), hawks (*Buteo* spp.), roadrunner (*Geococcyx californianus*), and turkey vulture (*Cathartes aura*). Occasionals include golden eagle (*Aquila chrysaëtos*) and sandhill crane (*Grus canadensis*).

Currently dominant land species include mule deer

(*Odocoileus hemionus*), coyote (*Canis latrans*), and bad-ger (*Taxidea taxus*). Since importation from arid north-ern Africa in 1957, the agile aoudad sheep (*Ammotragus lervia*) has made the canyons home.

Archeology: Fieldwork, carried out predominantly by per-sonnel from West Texas State University at Canyon, has identified several hundred archeological sites in the general area of the park. By far the majority of those reported sites have been ephemeral and as yet have not been further investigated. Although the sites represent all the periods of Texas archeology, the Lake Theo Fol-som Site is the most significant site yet known in the park, and it provides the central topic of the remainder of this chapter.

From the dam, the Lake Theo Site is visible to the west at the opposite end of the lake. It and the Lubbock Lake Site are the only Folsom sites open to the public in Texas. The Lake Theo Site is a typical example of what is known about the Folsom hunters. They depended on a large, now extinct form of buffalo (*Bison antiquus*). Kill sites where buffalo were stampeded into a ravine, surface finds, rockshelters, and open campsites are all known in Texas, but clear, well-defined Folsom butchering and camp sites are rare. This site may turn out to be one of the most significant Paleoindian sites in North America.

The Lake Theo Folsom Site was reported by an amateur archeologist in 1972, thereby emphasizing once again the importance of amateurs in modern archeology. Sub-sequent excavations revealed at least two buried bone beds associated with Paleoindian points and other ar-tifacts, many attributed to the Folsom Complex. The Paleoindian occupation area is thought to measure at least 250 feet by 210 feet, or about 52,500 square feet. Only a fraction of the area has been excavated, since the Paleoindian component is buried under 6 to 8 feet of deposits. As of this writing, only about 4,500 cubic feet have been removed.

According to the excavators' interpretation, this site represents a base camp where Folsom hunters repeatedly brought bison carcasses for butchering. The bison were probably trapped and killed in one of the many arroyos and box canyons in the area. A preponderance of certain bones and the absence of others suggests that legs, ribs, and rear portions of the animals were transported, while the remainder of the animal was left at the kill site. A preponderance of bones of young animals has suggested that only younger animals were selected for the kill. Another explanation is that although other, presumably older and tougher animals may have been killed, only the younger ones were butchered and brought back to camp. That possibility has exciting implications. Perhaps these hunters were practicing what may have led to domestication in other places, at other times, and with other species: they kept a herd captive in the nearby canyons and killed only the young. Such practices have been shown elsewhere as a strong factor in the gradual evolution of wild species into domestic forms. As yet, this is mere speculation as far as the Lake Theo Site is concerned, but it is an idea that can be tested by further work.

One startling suggestion has already emerged from excavations at Lake Theo: "Evidence suggests that prior to final processing, a religious tribute was constructed in the bottom of a shallow gully in the form of vertically placed bison mandible halves and limb bones, arranged in a circle and buried in a shallow pit. As the butchering progressed, the bones were randomly thrown on top of and around the tribute until it was completely covered. The small gully was eventually filled with discarded bones. Their work finished, the hunters and their families left the area. Hide preparation, meat-drying, feasting and tool-making were major activities conducted by these people who later became identified as Folsom" (Harrison and Killen 1978:89).

The feature described above consisted of "three left mandible halves [bison], a left and right tibia, a right femur, and a thoracic vertebral spine which had been placed in a small round hole with the distal ends at the bottom. Only the femur was placed proximal end first"

(Harrison and Killen 1978:20). It is the best evidence of some sort of early religious behavior we have been so far able to document in the New World. If accompanying evidence can be found to support the initial interpretation, the Lake Theo Site would immediately become the most spectacular early human occupation site in North America.

Another interesting aspect of this find is that it was accidental, or rather serendipitous. As is so often the case in important discoveries, it involved an element of chance. In removing a large block of the fossil bones for display purposes, the fieldworkers unknowingly cut through the ritual bones. The ritual arrangement of bones was not noticed until the block was uncovered in the lab. Even the most meticulous fieldwork (perhaps especially the most meticulous) is characterized by unexpected discovery of this sort. The trick is to recognize significance at some point.

Further Reading

Mercado-Allinger, P. 1982. Archeological investigations at 41Bl452 Caprock Canyons State Park, Briscoe County, Texas. Austin: Texas Parks and Wildlife Department. This is a report of a limited testing in July 1980 of a small site near the Lake Theo spillway. It is a good example of typical, modern conservation archeology work, and it is recommended for that reason.

Harrison, Billy R., and Kay L. Killen. 1978. Lake Theo: A stratified, early man bison butchering and camp site, Briscoe County, Texas. *Archeological Investigations, Phase II*. Canyon: Panhandle-Plains Historical Museum. This report, containing a description of the interesting bone offering at Lake Theo, is quite good but limited. The work reported here shows promise and is worthy of a well-funded, more comprehensive excavation in the near future.

Clovis Site
Blackwater Draw, Locality No. 1
Blackwater Draw Museum
Eastern New Mexico University
Portales, New Mexico 88130
(505) 562-2202

General description: The Clovis Site lies on private property along Blackwater Draw, north of Portales, New Mexico. It has been extensively quarried for several decades, and no archeological material remains. The Blackwater Draw Museum of Eastern New Mexico University, in the vicinity of the original Clovis Site, is north of Portales on the road to Clovis (U.S. 70) and is easily reached from either city. A number of artifacts from the Clovis Site as well as other important sites in the Blackwater Draw and elsewhere in eastern New Mexico may be viewed in interpretive displays, along with murals and fossil bones of mammoth and bison. Appropriate literature is available. The museum is easily visited, although the hours of operation are somewhat erratic. The hours generally include daytimes when the university is in session. Donations accepted.
   Altitude: 4,080 feet above mean sea level
   Average annual precipitation: 17.5 inches
   Average January minimum temperature: 20°F
   Average July maximum temperature: 92°F

Standard archeological interpretation:
   Site: Clovis Site (Blackwater Draw No. 1)
   Type of site: Open camp
   Developmental stage: Hunting and gathering
   Archeological period: Paleoindian
   Dates: 10,000–8000 B.C.
   Archeological culture: Clovis Complex (type site); Folsom Complex
   Diagnostic traits: *Clovis* fluted points, mammoth remains; *Folsom* fluted points, *Bison antiquus* remains

Comment: Although most of the material that was of interest to archeology has been removed by quarrying activities, a visit to the area can be instructive. Even though it lies outside Texas, it is important to the archeology of the state in at least two respects. Historically, the site was one of those of primary importance in establishing that North America had been occupied by human populations at the same time that large Ice Age animals lived here. It is the first site where *Clovis* points were found in undeniable association with mammoth remains. It is the type site of the Clovis Complex and an important precursor to the Lubbock Lake Site in the history of the development of our modern concepts of early human occupation in the New World. In addition, water wells dug at this site are the earliest known wells of their type in the New World (Fig. 7).

The Clovis Site is also included here to emphasize the importance of preservation. It is a prime example of those types of sites that we seek to preserve today. In many respects, this was perhaps the most significant Early Man site in the United States, yet it was deliberately destroyed. Under modern standards in Texas, the site likely would have been preserved, but conditions in New Mexico were not favorable for preservation. Now, it is too late; preservation at the Clovis Site is no longer feasible. Fortunately, the Lubbock Lake Site, similar to the Clovis Site in many respects, has been preserved and is open and easily accessible to interested visitors.

Environment: The Clovis Site (Fig. 3) is situated within the northwestern corner of the Llano Estacado (Staked Plains). This region, with an average elevation of more than 4,000 feet, is the highest region on the entire Llano. The environment is similar to that of the rest of the Llano, which is described in the Lubbock Lake section of this book.

The Clovis Site itself (Blackwater Draw No. 1), on Blackwater Draw some 90 miles northwest of its juncture with

Yellowhouse Draw at Lubbock, is the best known of many similar sites in this area of the Llano Estacado. Although similar, it differed in at least one important respect. Major freshwater springs emerged here and provided an apparently stable water source for long periods. Other sites in the Llano area seem to have been more ephemeral in their occupation. People returned to the Clovis Site time and again for several thousand years, and the springs seem to have been the major attraction. In that sense, the Clovis Site may be similar to the site at Aquarena Springs, described elsewhere in this volume.

Archeology: Two important things illustrated by the Clovis Site are discussed here. The first is the concept of a type site. The second is the stratigraphy of the site and the use of a highly stylized representation of stratigraphic observations.

The Concept of a Type Site
   When archeologists refer to a site as a type site, they usually mean that the site in question was the most important source of artifacts for a named artifact type or cultural complex. Often, the first site where an artifact type or complex is discovered and recognized becomes known as the type site. For example, some of the earliest systematic archeological excavations in Europe were carried out in a rockshelter site overlooking the small village of Le Moustier in southwestern France. Artifacts from certain strata there were found to be associated with Neanderthal remains. Those artifact types have come to be definitive of the Moustierian culture. Le Moustier, therefore, is the type site of the Moustierian culture.
   In the same sense, the Clovis Site is the type site for the Clovis Complex, a prehistoric cultural complex first identified here, near Clovis, New Mexico. Other type sites in this area include the Folsom Site near Folsom, New Mexico, type site of the Folsom Complex, and the Plainview Site near Plainview, Texas, type site of the *Plainview* point

Stratigraphy at the Clovis Site

Figure 7 is a stylized drawing from field notes and sketches made during a visit to the site in 1968. The observations that served as the basis for the notes and sketches were made at several stratigraphic sections that had been cleared along the south side of the quarry, an area that has subsequently been removed. In fact, if the same section coordinates were located today, they would be suspended in the air, since quarrying operations have substantially lowered the floor of the quarry. The strata represented a compressed section of strata found elsewhere in the site. The following descriptions are a compendium of information from the references listed for this chapter as well as on-site observations.

Stratum A. This is the gravel bedrock upon which the occupied strata rested. The gravel was the focus of the quarrying operations. Radiocarbon dates of about 15,500 years ago suggest these gravels are part of a deposit known to geologists as the Tahoka formation. Remains of mammoth, horse, and a now extinct form of buffalo (*Bison antiquus*) have been reported from this unit. No evidence of human occupation is known from this or lower strata.

Stratum B. This unit is composed of two distinct parts. The lower, and presumably older, is a gray sand (B1) radiocarbon dated at about 11,600 years ago, and the upper member is a brown, spring-laid sand (B2) with a radiocarbon date of about 11,200 years ago. (The "brown sand wedge" interfingers with the gray sand, into which it was introduced by spring action.) Radiocarbon dates of about 11,500 years ago have been consistently reported for stratum B.

Although there is a continuing controversy concerning the proper dating and interpretation of the two parts of this layer, the gray-brown sand unit is widely recognized as containing some of the most reliable evidence for the earliest known human occupation in the New World. The gray sand unit at the Clovis Site was the first unit in which *Clovis* points were associated with mammoth remains. Stratum B is thus one of the most impor-

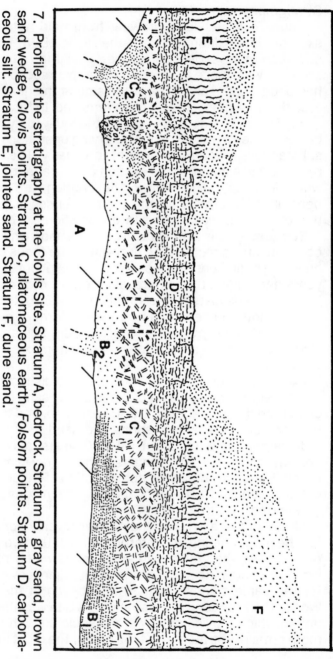

7. Profile of the stratigraphy at the Clovis Site. Stratum A, bedrock. Stratum B, gray sand, brown sand wedge, *Clovis* points. Stratum C, diatomaceous earth, *Folsom* points. Stratum D, carbonaceous silt. Stratum E, jointed sand. Stratum F, dune sand.

tant of all stratigraphic units at all sites in the United States.

Stratum C. This unit is separated from stratum B by what geologists call an erosional disconformity. The term is descriptive in the sense that there is evidence (indicated in the drawing by an indistinct, undulating line) of an erosional period between the deposition of stratum B and the subsequent deposition of stratum C. Unknown quantities of deposits were removed during this erosional interval.

Stratum C is well known to students of early human occupation as the diatomaceous stratum, because it has a high concentration of fossil diatom skeletons as a major component of the matrix (indicated in the drawing by short, paired lines at various angles to one another). Diatoms are small colonial or planktonic algae with skeletons that contain silicon. They thrive in certain types of ponds, and it is possible to determine characteristics of a pond by identifying diatoms from it. Large concentrations of diatom skeletons produce diatomite, a light, gray to white, sparkling substance often used in filtering elements. Diatomite is found in parts of stratum C, but the stratum is characterized by a mixture of diatoms, sand, and silt called diatomaceous earth.

This deposit contained the remains of *Bison antiquus* in association with *Folsom* fluted points. Radiocarbon dates have been quite consistent at about 10,000 years ago. The Clovis Site is one of the increasing number of sites where both the Clovis Complex and the Folsom Complex have been found. The Lubbock Lake Site is another.

Stratum D. This unit is characterized by a clayey, dark, fine sandy silt. Sometimes referred to as a carbonaceous silt, this stratum overlies the diatomaceous earth of stratum C with only a slight erosional disconformity between. As shown in the drawing, the upper portion of this stratum is marked by mud cracks filled with calcareous wedges, indicating that ponding intervals alternated with long, dry periods when the pond dried and deep cracks

formed in the muddy silt. The cracks were subsequently filled with calcium-bearing deposits.

Bison antiquus has been reported in this layer in association with Paleoindian points similar to *Plainview,
Eden, Scottsbluff,* and *Sandia.* The artifacts, radiocarbon
dated to about 8,000 or 9,000 years ago, have been locally assigned to the Portales Complex.

Stratum E. Separated from the carbonaceous silt of
stratum D by a marked erosional disconformity, this unit
has been described as a red, jointed sand. The term
"jointed" in this context simply refers to the joints formed
in this hard, sandy deposit. Remains of modern animals
and Archaic cultures have been discovered in this unit.
Stratum E has been carbon dated to about 5,000 years
ago and is thought to be the local representation of a
long dry interval known as the Altithermal that affected
the entire southwestern region of North America (perhaps
all of the northern hemisphere) immediately before the
onset of the modern climatic regime.

A rather spectacular feature associated with this unit
is a number of wells dug from the eroded surface of the
jointed sand into lower levels. A stylized example of such
a well appears just to the right of spring C2 in Figure 7.
These wells indicate a period of relatively little moisture
during which people were forced to dig for their water.
The wells are the earliest known in the New World.

Stratum F. This unit, lying disconformably upon the
jointed sand, is composed of tan, eolian (windblown) dune
sand. The cross-bedding that is typical of dunes is
represented by units of stipples. Today, this unit is easily observed as the active, partially stabilized sand dunes
that dominate the landscape between Portales and Clovis. Relatively recent prehistoric materials, projectile
points and sherds, as well as historic materials and
modern animal remains have been found in this deposit.

Further Reading

Hester, J. J. 1972. *Blackwater Locality No. 1: A Stratified, Early Man Site in Eastern New Mexico.* Fort Burg-

win Research Center, Publication No. 8. Dallas: Southern Methodist University. At the time of its publication, this was the most important single source dealing with the Clovis Site. There is an excellent summary of work at this important site, good illustrations, and a bibliography. Highly recommended, but difficult to find.

Wendorf, D. F. (assembler). 1961. *Paleoecology of the Llano Estacado.* Fort Burgwin Research Center, Publication No. 1. Santa Fe: Museum of New Mexico Press. A number of excellent studies directed toward an understanding of late Pleistocene changes in the environment of the Llano are presented here. Recommended.

Lubbock Lake Landmark State Historic Site
Texas Tech Museum
4th and Indiana
Lubbock, Texas 79408
(806) 742-2479

General description: The Lubbock Lake Landmark, in the far northwestern corner of Lubbock, is just north of the intersection of Loop 289 and U.S. 84 (Clovis Road). This park consists of the banks and channel of a portion of an archaic meander of Yellowhouse Draw, a tributary of the upper Brazos River. During a dredging operation by the WPA in the thirties, bones of extinct animals were recognized. Throughout the succeeding five decades repeated excavations have produced an impressive record of geological and archeological interest.

A casual visitor today sees dense growths of salt cedar, elm, and weeds and trash inside a fenced section of the draw that was excavated about fifty years ago to deepen the shallow draw to form a small reservoir. Approaching the buildings and excavations of the landmark, a visitor will typically begin to sense the significance of the site. It is difficult to put into objective terms, but the feeling springs from the realization that this is a specific place where human beings can be shown to have been living for about 12,000 years. That sensation cannot be recaptured in museum demonstrations or replications.

At the time of this writing approximately 300 acres have been designated a state historic site and will be developed in the years ahead to be more accessible to the general public year-round. At the present, access is primarily during the summer months when the various digs are under way, and guided tours are offered Saturday mornings at nine. Visits at other times may be arranged through the Texas Tech Museum.

Altitude: 3,100 feet above mean sea level
Average annual precipitation: 18.5 inches
Average January minimum temperature: 25°F
Average July maximum temperature: 92°F

Standard archeological interpretation:
Site: Lubbock Lake
Type of site: Open camp
Developmental stage: Hunting and gathering
Archeological period: Paleoindian
Dates: 10,000–8000 B.C.
Archeological culture: Clovis Complex; Folsom Complex
Diagnostic traits: *Clovis* fluted points, mammoth remains; *Folsom* fluted points, *Bison antiquus* remains

Comment: Perhaps more than any other locality, Lubbock Lake provides sites spanning the entire spectrum of human occupation of the Southern Plains. For the patient visitor, few other localities offer so much. In spite of recent improvements, this place requires a lot of work on the part of the visitor to be appreciated. Don't come expecting a sudden revelation, but look for new insights on each repeat trip. This description concentrates on two spectacular features: stratigraphy and the reconstruction of climates of the recent past.

Environment: Lubbock Lake Landmark is near the eastern edge of the Llano Estacado. (The name is often translated "staked plain," from a manner of trail marking by early Spanish explorers.) The Llano Estacado, a southern extension of the High Plains, is bounded in the north by the Canadian River. A thousand-foot escarpment called the Caprock forms the eastern margin. To the west the Llano is separated from the mountains by the valley of the Pecos River, and to the south it gradually merges with the Edwards Plateau. The edge of the latter is marked by the Balcones Escarpment.

It is easy to understand why early explorers needed to mark their trail along the way. The Llano Estacado is one of the flattest areas of the world. There are no tall landforms to serve as landmarks, few trees, and no flowing streams except for short periods after local rainstorms. Then streams are formed in the draws, and thousands of slight depressions form shallow, saline ponds. A few of the ponds, or playas ("playa" is Spanish for "beach," a reference to sandy mounds frequently deposited by the wind at the perimeter of the depressions), are quite large and have water year-round. Although the surface seems flat, it is actually more nearly like a tilted plane, with the higher elevations in the northwest at about 4,800 feet above sea level down to about 2,600 feet in the southeast. The average slope is about 9 feet per mile. On maps you can see that all the rivers drain toward the east or southeast.

Yellowhouse Draw, the major topographic feature of the Lubbock Lake Landmark, is an extinct branch of the upper Brazos River drainage. Before the earliest human occupation of this region, the Pecos River captured the east-flowing waters from the Sangre de Cristo Mountains of New Mexico. That exotic source supplied most of the water to cut the channel of Yellowhouse Draw. The capture of the headwaters of the Brazos, sometimes referred to in more vivid metaphor as a "beheading," greatly increased the flow of the Pecos while reducing the flow of Yellowhouse to its present dependence on local rainfall. One result of the change has been the formation of the modern small, shallow ponds along the draw. The former wider, deeper Yellowhouse Canyon has been mostly filled with recent sediments in distinct layers. The presence and accessibility of the layers (strata) are major factors in the archeological significance of this locality.

Climate. The modern climate of the Llano is characterized by extremes. I have seen the temperature plunge from the low seventies to near zero in several hours. Winds are strong and constant and remind one of that old joke in which the newcomer, bothered by the wind, asks, "Does the wind always blow this way?" To which the old-time resident responds, "No, sometimes it blows the other way." Prevailing winds are from the south and southeast, with occasional severe dust storms from the west and northwest.

Summertime temperatures are hot; the normal maximum daytime temperature is in the nineties, with frequent days over 100. Summer nights, because of the low humidity, cool rapidly to a normal low in the sixties. The coldest winter months have temperatures in the fifties, with frequent blue northers, when the temperature plunges into the low teens and occasionally hits zero and lower.

Modern precipitation averages from about 22 inches in the northeastern extremes of the Llano to about 14 inches in the southwestern portion. Because most of the precipitatii occurs in the summer, when the evaporation rate is highest, the effective annual precipitation is far lower than the average would suggest. An additional factor is the tendency for half or more of the year's precipitation to fall within a few hours during a cloudburst of hail and rain accompanied by high wind, lightning, and thunder. Violent flooding often results, as the water rushes into the arroyos and on downstream into the Brazos and other rivers. Thus much of the moisture is lost as runoff, lowering the effective annual precipitation still more.

Plants. Medium and short grasses are modern characteristic plant types throughout the Llano. Typical grasses include buffalo grass (*Buchloë dactyloides*), blue grama (*Bouteloua gracilis*), and Indian grass (*Sorghastrum nutans*). Early settlers reported grasses such as big bluestem (*Andropogon gerardii*) and little bluestem (*Schizachyrium scoparium*) that were as high as a horseback rider. Those grasses, though still present, are nowhere so tall or dense today. For the most part, trees are confined to drainages and escarpment areas and include mesquite (*Prosopis glandulosa*), juniper (*Juniperus pinchotii* and *J. monosperma,* both locally known as cedar), occasional cottonwood (*Populus sargentii*), and elm (*Ulmus* spp.).

Animals. Several animals that are characteristic of the modern environment on the Llano include the prairie dog (*Cynomys ludovicianus*), coyote (*Canis latrans*), and burrowing owl (*Speotyto cunicularia*). One of the most characteristic of modern plains animals, the buffalo (*Bison bison*), no longer roams free and, except for a few privately held animals and those in zoos, is gone from the Southern Plains.

Archeology: As mentioned above, one of the outstanding features of this locality is the accessibility of well-defined strata. The study of the stratigraphy of a site is the most powerful concept of modern geology and archeology. Stratigraphy offers both a basis for the association of various facts and a technique for dating that forms the basis for most of the other techniques. Without this technique, it is hard to imagine a modern science of geology or archeology. In fact, we probably wouldn't have our modern concept of time if the study of stratigraphy had not begun in the mid-nineteenth century.

Stratigraphy is simple and elegant, and therein lies its power. Given a series of strata, or layers, those near the bottom are older than those above them. And all else being equal, items found in the same stratum are associated more closely with one another than with items in other strata. Thus in the three strata represented in Figure 8, the lowest, stratum A, is the oldest, stratum C is the most recent, and stratum B, temporally as well as physically, separates the two. Furthermore, items x and y are associated with one another and are of relatively the same age since they are both in stratum A, and items n and o are similarly associated with one another and are of about the same age. This example is especially strong because stratum B contains no items; that is, stratum B is sterile in terms of those kinds of items. The argument that items x and y are older than items n and o is therefore stronger than it would be if stratum B contained items n, o, x, and y. Lubbock Lake Landmark is so important largely because it has such strong stratigraphy.

The simple concept of stratigraphy and its implications for the concept of time were not part of the worldview of Western Civilization until late in the eighteenth and early in the nineteenth centuries. Then, largely through the work of British geologists, a previously truncated view of the earth's past began to be replaced by a time frame of vastly greater proportions. The new image of the enormous depth of time, along with accumulating evidence of geologic process, was a major factor in the emergence of modern geology. As the ideas filtered through Western culture, they were eventually applied to determine the antiquity of humanity, and the foundation of the modern science of archeology was formed in Europe and the United States. The contribution of stratigraphy to archeology can hardly be exaggerated.

Although the concept is simple, its application is most often quite difficult. Even the basic assumption is not always correct. Sometimes a reverse stratigraphy is encountered, so the lowest elements represent the most recent depositions. That is unusual; a more common circumstance is a jumbled, mixed situation that requires skill and patience to collect and sort out the various threads of information. Even in geology, where normally the strata are relatively large, the problems are complex. In archeology the problems tend to be compounded by the complexities of microstratigraphy, the science of detecting, recording, and interpreting slight stratigraphic variations. Hence the significance of Lubbock Lake Landmark: the stratigraphy here is relatively clear-cut, the data are abundant, the site is accessible, and, perhaps most significant to anthropological archeology, evidence of human occupation can be found in stratigraphic context.

STRATUM C	
Item N	Item O
STRATUM B	
STRATUM A	
Item X	Item Y

8. Stylized representation of stratigraphy.

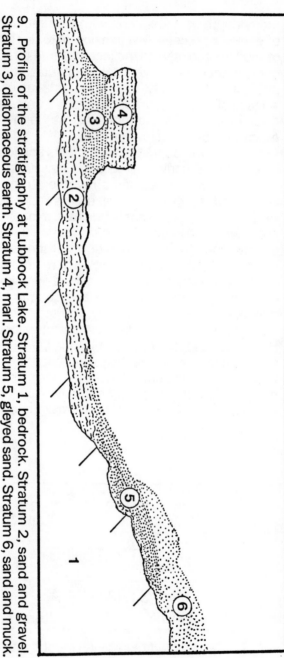

9. Profile of the stratigraphy at Lubbock Lake. Stratum 1, bedrock. Stratum 2, sand and gravel. Stratum 3, diatomaceous earth. Stratum 4, marl. Stratum 5, gleyed sand. Stratum 6, sand and muck.

Stratigraphy of Lubbock Lake Landmark

A stylized stratigraphic profile of a cross section at Lubbock Lake is presented in Figure 9. Essentially, five stratigraphic units have been identified as significant. They represent deposits that were made near the end of the Pleistocene glacial interval known as the Wisconsin in North America as well as subsequent deposits until the present.

Stratum 1: Bedrock. Usually assigned to the Blancan formation of Early Pleistocene age, this formation is well over a million years old and forms the basic structure of Lubbock Lake and Yellowhouse Draw.

Stratum 2: Sand and gravel (12,500–11,000 years ago). Characterized by sand in the lower portion, this stratum grades to a mixture of coarser sand and gravel in the upper portion. Judging from the nature of the material and apparent mode of deposition, the unit was probably deposited by a perennially flowing stream whose headwaters must have been some distance away. Artifacts of the Paleoindian Clovis Complex are associated in this bed with extinct species such as mammoth (*Elephas* spp.), stilt-legged horse (*Equus scotti*), and camel (*Camelops* spp.).

Stratum 3: Diatomaceous earth (11,000–10,000 years ago). The name for this stratum is derived from its high proportion of remains of silicon-containing, single-cell organisms known as diatoms. Diatomaceous units in this stratum form quite apparent gray to almost white bands and provide a handy fossil marker to the unit. Diatoms are generally associated with ponds rather than streams, and their presence suggests that the flowing stream represented by materials in stratum 2 has been replaced by a ponding interval in Yellowhouse Draw. Artifacts of the Paleoindian Folsom Complex have been found in this stratum with numerous extinct buffalo (*Bison antiquus*) that appear to have been butchered.

Stratum 4: Marl (10,000–7,000 years ago). This stratum is relatively sterile and forms a useful separation between the Paleoindian and more recent occupations of the locality. It possibly represents an interval in which the area was so inhospitable that it was untenable for humans. Or, since by that time many Pleistocene animals such as the horse, mammoth, and camel had become extinct in North America, perhaps those cultures that depended on the larger Pleistocene animals had not yet adapted to the changing environment.

Stratum 5: Gleyed sand (7,000–4,000 years ago). The unusual name was suggested by the characteristic gray, gray-green, and bluish colors found in this unit. The colors are the result of a chemical reaction in which oxygen was drawn from iron compounds in the mainly eolian (wind-blown) sandy deposits. Yellow and brown inclusions give the stratum a distinctive mottled look. Artifacts of various Archaic cultures in association with modern buffalo (*Bison bison*) have been recovered from this stratum. The upper part represents the formation of a paleosol (ancient soil) that has been described as the best post-Pleistocene soil on the Llano.

Stratum 6: Sand and muck (4,000 years ago until the present). That rather colorful name refers to the alternating conditions of relatively brief wet and dry intervals as the environmental circumstances approach those of today. By the beginning of deposition of this stratum, modern plant and animal communities had appeared. Artifacts characteristic of Late Prehistoric cultures are found in the lower parts of the unit, and the upper parts have elements of Protohistoric and Historic cultures associated with horses brought from Europe.

Reconstruction of Past Climates of the Llano

Data accumulated from a number of localities on the Llano permit certain generalizations about the past environment of the region. Such studies of the ancient environment, sometimes referred to as paleoecology, have given us a pretty good idea of what life on the Llano was like in the past. One aspect of paleoecology is climate. Information from the fields of paleontology (study of ancient animals), palynology (analysis of ancient pollen), and soil science offers evidence that the climate of the recent prehistoric past was remarkably different.

The trend has been from a relatively wet, cool climate in earliest Paleoindian times to the warm, dry semidesert conditions of today. There have been three major climatic intervals on the Llano since the earliest known human populations appeared: the San Jon Pluvial, the Altithermal, and the Medithermal.

San Jon Pluvial. Evidence for this interval is found in strata 2, 3, and 4 at Lubbock Lake. It represents an environment that at the beginning was cool and moist, a completion of the Ice Age environment in North America.

Pollen analysis of samples from stratum 2 indicates that the Llano was about ten degrees cooler than today and the precipitation was much higher. During this period a stream was flowing in the Yellowhouse Draw, and the Llano was like an open parkland with clusters of pine forest and perhaps even a few scattered spruce trees. The earliest known human populations, represented by the Clovis Complex at Lubbock Lake, hunted large Pleistocene animals such as mammoth and horse.

By the middle of the San Jon Pluvial, stratum 3, the climate had moderated somewhat, and ponds had replaced the stream flowing through the draw as precipitation decreased. Diatoms flourished in the still, sometimes brackish water; large animals such as the mammoth became extinct, while the people represented by the Folsom Complex hunted *Bison antiquus*.

Finally, in the last phase of the Ice Age environments, the marl characteristic of stratum 4 was formed. Many of the remaining Pleistocene species became extinct, while the general environment came to resemble a cool, sagebrush-dominated prairie. There is no evidence of human occupation at Lubbock during this interval.

Altithermal. This term refers to a sometimes controversial post-Pleistocene period in which the temperatures were significantly warmer than today's. At Lubbock Lake the Altithermal is represented by stratum 5. During this interval the climate was not only much warmer but also fluctuated from dry to relatively moist conditions. A result was the formation of the gleyed sands, a combination of windblown depositions. The period ends with the stabilization of the deposits and the formation of an organically rich soil, indicative of a return to moist conditions. Peoples of Archaic cultures hunted modern species including buffalo and deer in a mixed grassland environment.

Medithermal. Beginning with the relatively wet environment at the end of the Altithermal, the environment of the Llano has become progressively drier, until today's conditions prevail. The horse was reintroduced by the Spanish, and overgrazing rapidly depleted the grass cover of the modern desert grasslands.

Further Reading

These publications are most useful in consideration of the Lubbock Lake Landmark and archeology of the Llano Estacado. They are not generally available but have been found in larger libraries or at the Texas Tech Museum. In addition, personnel at the landmark will provide brochures and up-to-date information upon request.

Black, C. C. (ed.). 1974. History and prehistory of the Lubbock Lake Site. *The Museum Journal* XV. Lubbock: West Texas Museum Association, Texas Tech University.

Green, F. E. 1962. The Lubbock Reservoir Site: 12,000 years of prehistory. *The Museum Journal* VI:83–123. Lubbock: West Texas Museum Association, Texas Tech University.

Hester, J. J. 1972. *Blackwater Locality No. 1: A Stratified, Early Man Site in Eastern New Mexico.* Fort Burgwin Research Center, Publication No. 8. Dallas: Southern Methodist University.

Johnson, E. (ed.). 1988. *Lubbock Lake: Late Quaternary Studies on the Southern High Plains.* College Station: Texas A&M University Press. This is the most up-to-date, authoritative volume concerning the archeology of Lubbock Lake. The editor has been the major explorer at the site for more than a decade, and this is the most comprehensive single source available. Recommended.

Wendorf, D. F. (assembler). 1961. *Paleoecology of the Llano Estacado.* Fort Burgwin Research Center, Publication No. 1. Santa Fe: Museum of New Mexico Press.

Wendorf, D. F., and J. J. Hester (assemblers). 1975. *Late Pleistocene Environments of the Southern High Plains.* Fort Burgwin Research Center, Publication No. 9. Dallas: Southern Methodist University.

CENTRAL PRAIRIES REGION

The northern boundary of this vast, poorly defined region extends eastward along the Red River valley from the Caprock to the beginning of the Pineywoods. Proceeding southward, it becomes narrower as it merges with the Hill Country and is pinched between the Balcones Escarpment and the Pineywoods. Finally, at about Austin, the region curves westward, looking on the map like the tail of a comma, and gradually plays out west of San Antonio (Fig. 10).

In terms of prehistoric archeology, this region has little to offer. There were few human inhabitants in these areas until very recent prehistoric times. Even then the Blackland Prairies and the eroded Rolling Hill Prairies, distinct subdivisions of the region, were largely devoid of human population.

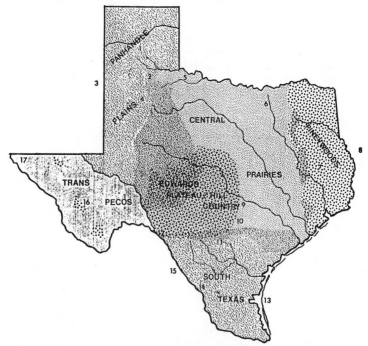

10. Central Prairies region. 5. Copper Breaks. 6. Lewisville.

It is hardly necessary to point out that this region is among the most heavily populated of any comparable region in modern Texas. Beginning in the late nineteenth century, the region became densely settled, and its population density has continued to increase rapidly. Although many recent historic sites, especially military posts, have been partially restored, relatively little archeological work is done at sites open to the public.

Although some important sites described in this book, such as McKinney Falls, Aquarena Springs, and San Antonio, are on the margin of this region, they possess characteristics of the adjacent Edwards Plateau and are included there rather than with other sites on the Central Prairies. Copper Breaks State Park and the Lewisville Site are the only two sites described in this region.

Copper Breaks State Park
Route 3
Quanah, Texas 79252
(817) 839-4331

General description: This state park is off Texas Highway 6 about halfway between Quanah (named for the
great Comanche leader Quanah Parker) and Crowell. Consisting of 1,933 acres of rolling, brushy plains, juniper
breaks, and grassy mesas, it offers an excellent interpretive center that includes details of the natural history of
the area as well as displays of artifacts, dioramas, paintings, and photographs interpreting the archeology of the
park. There are swimming, fishing, and boating facilities;
self-guided nature and hiking trails; picnicking and camping areas; and restroom and shower facilities. Reserva-
tions may be made up to 90 days in advance. Park
headquarters is open from 9 A.M. to 5 P.M. daily. Standard
state park fees.
   Altitude: 1,450 feet above mean sea level
   Average annual precipitation: 24 inches
   Average January minimum temperature: 28°F
   Average July maximum temperature: 99°F

Standard archeological interpretation:
   Site: Various
   Type of site: Open camps
   Developmental stage: Hunting and gathering; Historic
   Archeological period: Archaic; Protohistoric; Historic
   Dates: 8000 B.P.–present
   Archeological culture: Various
   Diagnostic traits: Various

Comments: This region must be what Larry McMurtry
had in mind when he wrote portions of *Lonesome Dove*.
The flat but rugged, wide-open country was the last out-
post for the North American bison and some free-ranging
Plains Indian groups such as the Kiowa and Comanche.
Cynthia Ann Parker, a real-life counterpart of McMurtry's

heroine, Lorena, was recaptured near the park south of the Pease River.

Environment: The park provides an excellent example of what has variously been called the Rolling Plains, Osage Plains, or Mesquite Plains. "Rolling Plains" is the term used here for the zone that includes the park. It is the westernmost of several distinct zones within the Central Prairies. Other zones in the region include the Eastern and Western Cross Timbers and the Blackland Prairie.

The geology of the park is characterized by Permian-age formations consisting mainly of shale, sandstone, siltstone, and dolomite interbedded with gypsum. Iron oxides in the formations are responsible for the predominant reddish color of the ground. The name "Copper Breaks" is thus quite descriptive of the general appearance of the park.

The major streams of the zone are tributaries of the Red River and the Brazos River. The Pease River, which forms part of the southern boundary of the park, joins the Red River about 40 miles to the east, and a point of the divide between the Red River basin and the Brazos basin lies at the town of Benjamin, about 50 miles south of the park. Although water is usually available, it is often "gyppy" from the dissolved deposits in the Permian redbeds and therefore not good to drink.

Plants. Mesquite (*Prosopis glandulosa*) dominates the modern plant community in the lowland flats, while mixed mesquite and juniper (*Juniperus* spp.) communities are characteristic of the upland mesas. Other plants include various grasses, prickly pear (*Opuntia phaeacantha*), pigweed (*Chenopodium leptophyllum, Amaranthus retroflexus*), milkweed (*Asclepias* spp.), and Russian thistle (*Salsola kali*).

Animals. More than 300 animal species have been identified in the park area in modern times. Most are birds, and many of them are migratory. Resident avian species include meadowlark (*Sturnella neglecta*), nighthawk (*Chordeiles minor*), scissortail (*Muscivora forfica-*

ta), and red-tailed hawk (*Buteo jamaicensis*). Mammals include spotted skunk (*Spilogale interrupta*), opossum (*Didelphis virginiana*), white-tailed deer (*Odocoileus virginianus*), and, until late in the nineteenth century, buffalo (*Bison bison*).

Archeology: A cultural sequence has not been well established for the Rolling Plains zone of the Central Prairies. Based on the relatively little work that has been carried out here, it seems that the area was never the site of large human occupation. Although all the periods of the Texas sequence are represented here, there is no evidence of either long or intense occupation. It seems that there has as yet been no time when this part of Texas has been especially attractive to human occupation.

Further Reading

Although there is not much readily available literature concerning the archeology of this part of Texas, the works by Suhm, Krieger, and Jelks (1954) and by Turner and Hester (1985), listed at the end of the introduction to Chapter 6, are useful for their descriptions of artifact types. In addition, the following reference is helpful but may be difficult to locate.

Etchieson, G. M., R. D. Speer, and J. T. Hughes. 1979. Archeological investigations in the Crowell Reservoir Area, Cottle, Foard, King, and Knox counties, Texas. Report prepared by the Archeological Research Laboratory, Kilgore Research Center, West Texas State University, Canyon. This monograph contains the results of archeological work done in the vicinity of Crowell Reservoir in an area immediately south of the Copper Breaks state park. It contains excellent summaries of the history, geology, and archeology of the area. Recommended.

Lewisville Site
Lewisville, Texas
No mailing address

General description: This site is usually submerged beneath the waters of Garza–Little Elm Reservoir near the juncture of Hickory Creek and the Elm Fork of the Trinity River northeast of the city of Lewisville. It is just east of a golf course and picnic area north of the west end of the dam at the reservoir, on property controlled by the U.S. Army Corps of Engineers, Fort Worth Division (Fig. 11). Although the area is easily accessible at most any time, the site itself cannot be seen. The edge of the water at the dam is within about 100 yards of the site at normal lake levels, and the undisturbed portions of the terrace give a good impression of the site habitat.
Altitude: 520 feet above mean sea level
Average annual precipitation: 33 inches
Average January minimum temperature: 34°F
Average July maximum temperature: 96°F

Standard archeological interpretation:
Site: Lewisville Site
Type of site: Open camp
Developmental stage: Hunting and gathering
Archeological period: Paleoindian
Dates: Late Ice Age
Archeological culture: Clovis Complex
Diagnostic traits: *Clovis* point

Comment: Although this site is currently covered by the waters of the Garza–Little Elm Reservoir, the shoreline near the site is easily accessible to those who are interested. The site is important as an excellent example of a type of site that suggests early human habitation in the New World. It is not much to look at for the casual visitor, but the true student of archeology will probably enjoy a visit. It has been among the most controversial of North American sites.

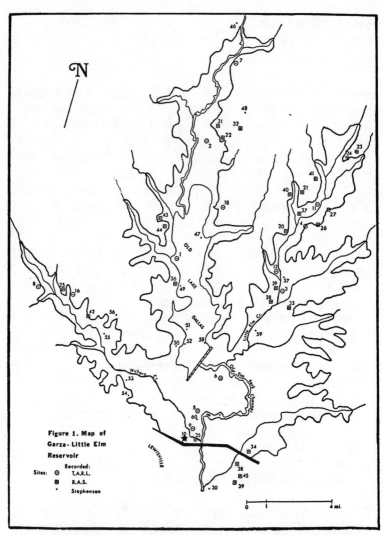

11. Garza–Little Elm Reservoir. The star marks the approximate location of the Lewisville Site. Numbers refer to the approximate location of other sites in the area.

Environment: The Trinity River forms a sharp boundary between the Eastern Cross Timbers zone and the Blackland Prairie zone in this area of the Central Prairies. Hickory Creek, joining the Trinity from the west, is entirely in the Eastern Cross Timbers. The Lewisville Site, just south of the junction of Hickory Creek and the Trinity, is similarly in the Cross Timbers. Across the river the Blackland Prairie extends eastward to the transition zone between the Central Prairies and the Pineywoods.

The Blackland Prairie is characterized by alkaline, black clay soils with a high organic content. The Blackland soils are heavy and difficult to cross when moist. The Eastern Cross Timbers zone is characterized by a sandy soil derived from the underlying Woodbine sandstone formation and is relatively well drained and easy to traverse when wet. Those characteristics are probably correlated with a human preference for sandy soil for occupation until very recent times.

Plants. Characteristic plants of the area include grasses such as little bluestem (*Schizachyrium scoparium*), Indian grass (*Sorghastrum nutans*), big bluestem (*Andropogon gerardii*), and speargrass (*Stipa leucotricha*). Mesquite (*Prosopis glandulosa*), oak (*Quercus* spp.), hackberry (*Celtis laevigata*), and slippery elm (*Ulmus rubra*) are dominant trees, and vines and shrubs include mustang grape (*Vitis mustangensis*), rusty blackhaw (*Viburnum rufidulum*), smooth sumac (*Rhus glabra*), and poison ivy (*Rhus toxicodendron*).

Animals. Year-round resident birds include turkey vulture (*Cathartes aura*), killdeer (*Charadrius vociferus*), mourning dove (*Zenaidura macroura*), and crow (*Corvus brachyrhynchos*). Common mammals include armadillo (*Dasypus novemcinctus*), pocket gopher (*Geomys bursarius*), and common mouse (*Mus musculus*).

Archeology: Since the site is covered by water almost all the time and therefore cannot be visited except under unusual circumstances, one may wonder why it is included in a guide to archeological sites. Quite simply, the Lewisville Site is perhaps the best archeological site of its type in Texas.

This type of site is frequently encountered and is often the center of controversy. It is the type of site that offers much promise, but it doesn't seem to work out. There are many such sites, and it is, of course, in the nature of things that many endeavors pursued with great expectations will fail to meet those expectations. In archeology, some of the highest hopes lie in the search for the earliest evidence of human presence in the New World. The Lewisville Site has offered evidence that it might be the one.

The site was discovered during construction in the early fifties, when dirt for the dam was being removed from the river terrace. Dragline operations revealed subsurface burned areas. Upon excavation and analysis, radiocarbon dates in excess of 38,000 years were reported in association with a *Clovis* point and other artifacts. There followed a period of considerable controversy, largely because the date of 38,000 years was incompatible with *Clovis* points, thought to be at most about 12,000 years old. The situation remained in archeological limbo until the lake level dropped precipitously in the late seventies and early eighties, exposing the site for the first time since the lake had been filled. It was then that a crew from the Smithsonian Institution excavated more of the burned areas. Trying to leave no doubt about their conclusions, the crew carefully screened through the burned areas. Again artifacts were found, and again a very old carbon date was attained. This time, however, evidence suggested that the very old date may have resulted from contamination by lignite or some other substance. Tentatively, the site is considered to be a Clovis site and may represent the earliest known use of fossil fuel. The excitement concerning the Lewisville Site continues, and so it is included here.

Further Reading

Crook, W. W., Jr., and R. K. Harris. 1957. Hearths and artifacts of early man near Lewisville, Texas, and associated faunal material. *Bulletin of the Texas Archeological Society* 28:7–97.

———. 1958. A Pleistocene campsite near Lewisville, Texas. *American Antiquity* 23(3):233–246. These two articles represent the initial reports of Clovis materials associated with Pleistocene terrace deposits in the Trinity River system near Lewisville. Recommended.

Heizer, Robert A., and R. A. Brooks. 1965. Lewisville— ancient campsite or wood rat houses? *Southwestern Journal of Anthropology* 21:155–165. This article is a classic example of the skepticism that has surrounded the Lewisville site. The authors develop and present an alternative explanation for the burned "hearths." Recommended.

PINEYWOODS REGION

This region represents a westward extension of the great forested areas of the eastern United States. Although physiographically much of the region is part of the coastal plain, parts of the northern extremes derive from the mountains of eastern Oklahoma and Arkansas. The area is loosely defined as that region of eastern Texas characterized by pine forests (Fig. 12).

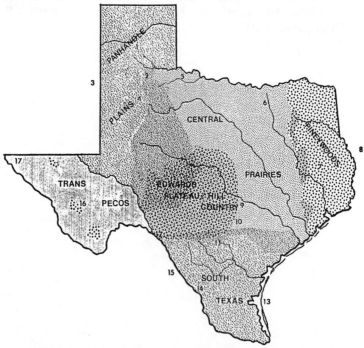

12. Pineywoods region. 7. Caddoan Mounds. 8. Los Adaes.

The Pineywoods was the most heavily occupied portion of the state during the Late Prehistoric period and has continued to be heavily occupied since. Before that time, there was only a relatively sparse population in this part of Texas. Two major archeological sites associated with Caddoan culture, one of the most successful Late Prehistoric and Early Historic cultures in the Pineywoods, are discussed in this section.

Caddoan Mounds State Historic Site
Route 2, Box 85C
Alto, Texas 75925
(409) 858-3218

General description: This site is 6 miles southwest of Alto, Cherokee County, on Texas Highway 21. Its 93.5 acres were acquired by the State in 1975 to protect and exhibit what is perhaps the most extensive Late Prehistoric site in Texas. An excellent interpretive center clearly explains the role of the site in the development of Caddoan culture and exhibits numerous artifacts from the

13. Caddoan house. This house was constructed as an experiment in archeology at Caddoan Mounds. (Drawing courtesy Texas Parks and Wildlife.)

site. The history of excavations at the site is presented and illustrated, and a beehive-shaped Caddoan house has been reconstructed (Fig. 13). Perhaps most interesting are three mounds conspicuously present on the otherwise flat bottomland of the Neches River. Guided tours are available. The park is open from 8 A.M. to 5 P.M. Wednesday through Sunday, closed Monday and Tuesday. Standard state park admission fees. Group tours by appointment.

Altitude: 255 feet above mean sea level
Average annual precipitation: 44 inches
Average January minimum temperature: 38°F
Average July maximum temperature: 91°F

Standard archeological interpretation:
Site: George C. Davis Site
Type of site: Village; ceremonial center
Developmental stage: Agricultural
Archeological period: Late Prehistoric
Dates: A.D. 800–A.D. 1200
Archeological culture: Alto Focus; Gibson Aspect; Late Mississippian
Diagnostic traits: Villages, mounds, ceramics, ground and polished stone tools, *Alba, Gary, Ellis, Wells* points

Comment: One of the persons most involved with this site, Dee Ann Story, wrote: "Of the thousands of known prehistoric sites in Texas few have attracted as much attention as the George C. Davis Site in the central portion of East Texas—one of the largest, continuously occupied (from *ca.* A.D. 700 to 1250) aboriginal settlements in the state. The site consists of an extensive village and three obvious man-made earthen mounds, remains which archeologists have identified as belonging to a distinctive and widespread cultural pattern known as Caddoan" (Story 1972:i).

Over the years many of the most distinguished amateurs and professionals in Texas have worked at this site. The park is truly a remarkable monument not only to the prehistoric peoples who lived here and originally built it but also to the modern people of Texas who have "lived" here and now share in its rebuilding.

Environment: The people who built the structures here, the Caddos, had a culture well adapted to a forested environment. The site, in the bottomland of the Neches River, lies at the western border of the Texas Pineywoods and is among the westernmost of any of the prehistoric woodland cultures. It is an excellent example of how important environmental variables can be in the geographic distribution of cultural traits.

Two categories important in archeological interpretation, the macroenvironment and the microenvironment, will be discussed here. Macroenvironment includes broad aspects of the environment such as climate, soils, geology, and regional plants and animals. Microenvironment, on the other hand, refers to more specific and local variations that are characteristic of a particular site. For example, at Caddoan Mounds the macroenvironment seems to be important in limiting the distribution of a distinctive culture. The Eastern Woodland culture is found in a variety of wooded environments but seems to be restricted by the natural limits of the forest. Specifically, the following woodland traits are among those limited by the change from forest to prairie: 1. Wood is used extensively for utensils and for construction of the built environment. 2. Lithic technologies using tough, resilient stone that must be shaped by pecking, grinding, and polishing and that are associated with woodworking are no longer necessary or feasible where there is no significant amount of wood. 3. Woodland farming practices seem to have been limited to available rainfall. Caddoan Mounds is at the western boundary of sufficient rainfall for woodland farming practices. 4. Sandy soils associated with much of the Eastern Woodland area were relatively easy to cultivate without a plow. The heavy sod of the Blackland Prairie was not amenable to prehistoric farming practices.

Different types of sites have been shown to be related to microenvironments within the larger context of vast forested areas. Caddoan Mounds provides an excellent example of a type of site found in similar microenvironments—rises or alluvial terraces above flat bottomland areas along rivers and streams—throughout the forests of the southeastern United States. The most spectacular site of this type is found in the American Bottoms, the bottomland microenvironment near the confluence of the Missouri and Mississippi rivers near present-day St. Louis, Missouri. There, a site named Cahokia Mounds, ← or simply Cahokia, with an estimated supporting population of about 30,000, was the largest prehistoric religious center north of Mexico. Approximately 120 mounds have been identified there. One, Monk's Mound, is the largest known prehistoric structure in the United States. Although Caddoan Mounds is much smaller than Cahokia, it offers an interesting glimpse of one of the most successful prehistoric cultures in the western hemisphere.

The Macroenvironment. The Texas Pineywoods represents a western extension of the Southern Pinelands, which begin in the pine barrens of New Jersey, extend south through the Atlantic states, west through the Gulf states to East Texas, and north along the Mississippi River and its tributaries. This vast forested area contains representatives of numerous biological communities typical of warm, relatively humid climates.

Plants. Longleaf (*Pinus palustris*), shortleaf (*Pinus echinata*), and loblolly (*Pinus taeda*) are dominant pines, and typical hardwoods include oak (*Quercus* spp.), elm (*Ulmus* spp.), and magnolia (*Magnolia* spp.). Grasses characteristic of the frequent open meadows include bluestems (*Andropogon* spp.), Indian grass (*Sorghastrum nutans*), and switch grass (*Panicum virgatum*).

Animals. Besides the ubiquitous white-tailed deer (*Odocoileus virginianus*), species characteristic of the Pineywoods include opossum (*Didelphis virginiana*), wild boar (*Sus scrofa*), gopher (*Geomys bursarius*), and gray squirrel (*Sciurus carolinensis*).

The Microenvironment. The site per se, that is, the village, the mounds, and immediately related elements of the built environment, lies on a southwest-trending ter-

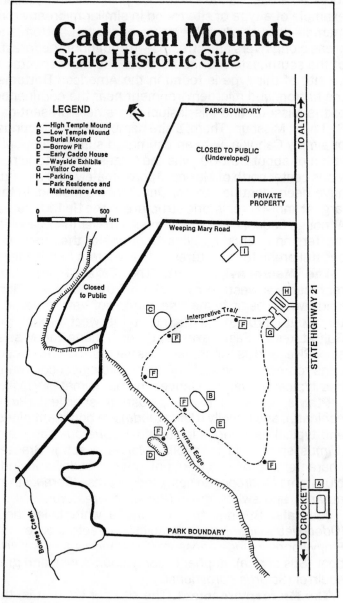

14. Caddoan Mounds. (Map courtesy Texas Parks and Wildlife.)

race remnant overlooking the floodplain bottomlands less than a mile northeast of the juncture of Bowles Creek with the Neches River (Fig. 14). When visiting the site, it is helpful to use the headquarters building as a point of reference.

The park headquarters is located within a major portion of the village, and Texas Highway 21 bisects the terrace remnant and the site. The tallest and northernmost of the three conspicuous mounds is the burial mound. About 200 yards southwest of it is a large, low-lying platform. Both these prominent features lie near the terrace edge overlooking Bowles Creek. The large mound across the highway lies due south of the burial mound. It was built farther from the terrace's edge than the other two mounds and can be clearly seen in the bottomland from either side of the terrace edge.

The creek enters the Neches three quarters of a mile southwest of the site, so the nearest source of water was the creek and not the river, an important point in understanding the proper context of the site with relation to the river bottomlands and the hilly uplands.

The terrace itself is about 50 feet above the bottomlands. That is important in terms of modern problems of excavation and interpretation as well as in terms of various explanations of prehistoric significance. Standard interpretation at the site and in the literature has been mostly concerned with prehistoric significance, but problems of excavation and interpretation are directly related to the microenvironment. Thus in archeological interpretation, not only must the general features of regional environment be taken into account but specific aspects of the local microenvironment must also be considered.

Archeology: One of the most common methods of interpretation in archeology is analogy. For example, if a particular tool looks like a knife, we call it a knife, and we thereby attribute to it all the meanings and usages such a designation implies. We assign the tool to the category "knife" based on some properties in the tool that we recognize as knifelike. In other words, we rely on our recognition of similarity to form an association between items, and then assign properties to the items based on the perceived similarity. That is interpretation by analogy.

Interpretation of that sort is tempting but often quite misleading. Although analogy in its many forms is one of the most common forms of reasoning, it can lead to inaccurate judgments about the nature of things. Its strength is in its ability to suggest comparisons, to point out possibilities, upon which explanations may be based. In that sense, analogy is merely the beginning, not the end, of interpretation.

Analogy is especially difficult to use in the interpretation of cultural materials. In archeology, the problem is compounded by the impossibility of asking the people involved whether our sense of the significance of their artifacts is valid. The problematic use of analogy is manifest at sites such as Caddoan Mounds.

Conspicuous sites such as Caddoan Mounds seem to demand explanation. In the normal course of events various speculations are offered with varying degrees of sophistication. Similarities are noted, and analogic interpretation runs amok. People who should know better are carried away with their favorite set of similarities and come to see still more similarities that even they couldn't see before. Although that is great fun, it often results in poor archeology.

In the case of Caddoan Mounds, many of the speculations have involved the prominent mounds. They have been identified with other, similar mounds in the Eastern Woodlands for a long time, but the nature of the relationship has remained problematic. There has been much speculation about the association of the mounds with a highly stratified, agricultural society, and about the striking similarities with sites elsewhere in the Caddoan area, the Mississippi drainage area in general, and in Mexico.

One of the most remarkable similarities with the Classical Period in Mexico was revealed by various excavations at Caddoan Mounds. The excavations repeatedly turned up evidence of a definite rhythm, a cycle, of construction and destruction that seems to be a local variation of the Mesoamerican concept of time. In Meso-america (that part of Mexico, Honduras, Belize, and Guatemala characterized by prehistoric development of writing, common architectural styles, agricultural prac-tices, and a host of other traits) time was of paramount significance. The Mesoamerican worldview featured cy-cles of time within cycles of time. One of the most im-portant cycles was a mystical period that consisted of ——— the last five days of each year. During these holy days, time was at a standstill, and all attention was focused on the ritual necessary to get the new cycle off to a good start. In a way it was a New Year's Eve ritual, but with a vengeance.

Two important Mesoamerican cycles—the 260-day year based on the cycles of the planet Venus and the 365-day solar year—coincided every 52 years. The five holy days at the end of every year were especially im-portant at the end of the last year in the 52-year cycle, so important that pots were broken, fires extinguished, sacrifices (including human lives) offered, new buildings initiated, and old structures refurbished. It was one of the most characteristic cycles celebrated throughout Mesoamerica. Excavations at Caddoan Mounds have re-vealed what appears to be a typically Mesoamerican se-ries of 52-year cycles. For example, the cemetery, Mound C, was found to have been built in six distinct stages. The following interpretation is given as an example of the way analogy can lead to a dramatic but unverified interpretation (illuminated interpretation based on Sto-ry 1972).

Construction Stage I, log temple stage. This stage marks the first clear evidence of the Mound Builders at Caddoan Mounds. Around A.D. 860, the site was dedicat-ed by the sacrifice and ritual burial of at least eight peo-ple. The large rectangular grave (approximately 25 feet long, 16 feet wide, and 12 feet deep), one of the first structures at the site, was dug from the original surface and was framed with a low-lying enclosure around the grave pit. After the remains and accompanying grave goods were placed in the grave, a log temple was erected over the grave. Thus ended the dedication of the site.

Construction Stage II, platform mound stage. After the construction activity of stage I, the grave was relatively untended, and the log temple collapsed. Early in stage II, the original grave was filled, and a flat-topped mound approximately 12 feet high and 75 feet in diameter was constructed directly over the original grave. At precisely the beginning of the first 52-year cycle since the site dedication, another series of ritual sacrifices and burials was carried out. The date was approximately A.D. 900.

At least four people were sacrificed and ritually buried in a grave dug into the flat surface atop the platform mound. The enormous rectangular grave measured 26 feet by 20 feet and was more than 16 feet deep. The remains were carefully arranged in the grave, and enormous quantities of grave offerings were included. A thin layer of sandy loam then carefully covered the remains and the most personal offerings. Ceremonial mats of cattail reeds were used to cover the contents of the lower part of the grave, and another, even more lavish assortment of offerings was placed in the upper part. In all, more than one thousand bits of ceremonial offerings have been identified from this burial. The grave was finally filled and sealed.

This period marked the zenith of occupation at Caddoan Mounds. No previous event had been and no subsequent ceremony would be so lavish as this. The date for this phase is uncertain but could be about A.D. 950. The event must have marked an exciting time for the people who lived in this tiny outpost of a New World civilization. Nothing like it would ever be seen here again.

Construction Stage III, red sandy clay stage. Once again, the burial area was left unattended for a time after the intense activity of construction. The sides of the mound eroded somewhat, and a veneer of sandy loam was applied. Near the end of the second complete

52-year cycle, the mound was enlarged to about 85 feet in diameter and raised to a height of 18 feet.

Sacrifices and ceremonial burials with ritual offerings once again began the new cycle. The overall impression is that the effort involved and the wealth displayed in this construction stage was significantly less than that of 52 years earlier. The date is about A.D. 1000.

Construction Stage IV, red and yellow silty loam stage. As another 52-year cycle came to an end, the population once again prepared the burial mound for its role in the rituals of renewal. The height of the mound was raised to about 20 feet, and the diameter was increased to more than 90 feet. Sacrifices were made and burials placed in graves in the mound. One of the graves, measuring 28 feet by 30 feet at the top with a depth of about 25 feet, is the largest known at the site. Grave offerings were rather meager. The construction dates from about A.D. 1050.

Construction Stage V, reddish brown and yellow loam stage. The height of the mound was raised to about 21 feet, and the diameter increased to 110 feet. Burials were no longer made from the upper elevation of the mound but were placed in graves dug from benches built on the flanks of the mound. Burials contained relatively few grave goods. The date is estimated to be approximately 1100.

Construction Stage VI, red sandy loam stage. This stage marked the final stage of construction at Caddoan Mounds. The site seems to have been abandoned shortly after one last series of human sacrifice and burial. In preparation for the ritual, the mound was enlarged to its final diameter of approximately 120 feet and raised to a height of almost 22 feet. Only one burial could be identified in this renewal cycle.

As is often the case in loose interpretations such as this, I have included enough descriptive facts to add a touch of authenticity, but it is also often the case that authors of this type of interpretation pay attention to fact only when it suits their case. An impressive and complicated site such as Caddoan Mounds presents almost irresistible temptations to stretch the evidence to fit an attractive analogy. Everybody believes something about such a site. Another special difficulty is that most sites in Texas—unlike many in Mexico, New Mexico, Arizona, and other parts of the world such as Stonehenge and Altamira—are relatively modest and do not strike the eye as quite so compelling as these mounds. Although the site is not nearly as spectacular as, say, Casa Grande in Arizona or Teotihuacán, that huge prehistoric city northeast of modern Mexico City, it is related to those sites in several ways: through the presence of monumental structures (those at Caddoan Mounds are modest but still impressive), through the similarities in sociocultural evolution suggested, and also more directly.

Standing on top of the burial mound and looking over the site, an archeologist will be tempted to recall the similarities between this site and many others in North America that can be related to spectacular developments in Mesoamerica. Those developments reached a zenith of sorts, similar to Classical Greek civilization in the Western tradition, about the time the occupation at Caddoan Mounds was getting under way in earnest. During that period, about A.D. 700–900, influences from the great culture centered about Teotihuacán were reaching throughout North America. In the Mississippi River system, the influences are collectively known as the Mississippian. They certainly reached the Caddoan area. The nature and the degree of the influence are open to question, but the pervasiveness of the similarities cannot be denied.

I like to think of the influence of that faraway cultural center as similar to the effect that Rome might have had on a remote settlement in Ireland during the reign of Emperor Hadrian. Indeed, the similarities are striking in many ways: Teotihuacán and Rome were both at the height of their expansion, their empires were relatively benign, cultures of both were widely emulated, religion and imperial rule were closely related, trade was extensive, each had a series of relatively wise rulers, and, alas, each was soon to suffer a series of disasters that led to their ultimate collapse.

Also, the people here at Caddoan Mounds were living a life in many ways similar to that enjoyed by our hypothetical Irish villagers at the height of Roman influence. No one has suggested, to my knowledge at least, that the similarity between life at Caddoan Mounds and life at a distant Irish village is more than can be explained in terms of parallel cultural evolution. There is no need to suggest a direct historic relationship between the Irish and the people at Caddoan Mounds; instead, the similarity can be explained in terms of similar stages of development.

But when the Caddoan Mounds Site is compared with areas in Mesoamerica, archeologists see so many similarities that they are tempted to say that there must have been some sort of Mesoamerican influence on the development at Caddoan Mounds, analogous to the relationship between the Irish village and Rome, as suggested above. It may yet be determined that there was such a relationship between the Caddoan area and Mesoamerica (certainly that seems likely), but there is no clear evidence of it at Caddoan Mounds.

Further Reading

Newell, H. P., and A. D. Krieger. 1949. The George C. Davis Site, Cherokee County, Texas. *Memoirs of the Society for American Archaeology,* No. 5.

Story, D. A. 1972. A preliminary report of the 1968, 1969, and 1970 excavations at the George C. Davis Site, Cherokee County, Texas. Report submitted to the Texas Historical Survey Committee, Austin.

Texas Parks and Wildlife Department. 1984. Caddoan Mounds: Temples and Tombs of an Ancient People. PWD Booklet 4000–384. Austin: Texas Parks and Wildlife Department.

Los Adaes State Commemorative Area and Los Adaes Tourist Information Center
Highway 6 West
Robeline, Louisiana 71469
(318) 472-6843

General description: This historical park lies about 80 miles southeast of Shreveport and immediately northeast of the town of Robeline, about halfway between Natchitoches (NAK-ah-tish) and Many (MAN-ney) (Fig. 15). The 14-acre Los Adaes State Commemorative Area has been marginally operated by the State of Louisiana since 1979. As of this writing, negotiations are under way to transfer operation of the site back to the Natchitoches Parish Police Jury (roughly the same as a county commissioners' court in Texas). At present the site may be visited between 8:30 A.M. and 5 P.M. seven days a week. Little interpretive material is available at the site, but plans include an on-site interpretive center.

Currently the Natchitoches Parish Police Jury operates a small interpretive center in Robeline. The address and telephone number listed above are for the Los Adaes Tourist Information Center. It is located in a small brown building about a mile from the site of Los Adaes and is open Tuesday through Saturday from 9 A.M. until 5 P.M. Since the status of Los Adaes is uncertain, be sure to call or write for current information before visiting this site.

Altitude: 480 feet above mean sea level
Average annual precipitation: 53 inches
Average January minimum temperature: 38°F
Average July maximum temperature: 94°F

Standard archeological interpretation:
Site: Presidio de Nuestra Señora del Pilar de los Adaes and Mission de San Miguel de los Adaes
Developmental stage: Agricultural, Historic
Archeological period: Protohistoric, Historic
Dates: A.D. 1720–1773
Archeological culture: Caddoan, Spanish colonial
Diagnostic traits: Native American artifacts such as

Natchitoches engraved and *Patton* engraved pottery and eighteenth-century historic artifacts

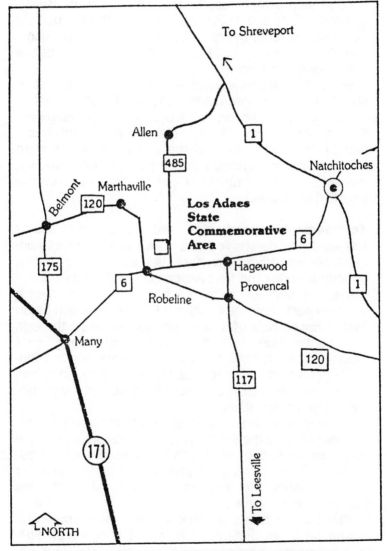

15. Los Adaes. (Map courtesy Louisiana State Bureau of Tourism.)

Comment: Although this site lies outside modern Texas, it is one of the most important sites in the Spanish colonial period of Texas history. Los Adaes, capital of the province of Texas and Coahuila for fifty years, was succeeded as provincial capital by San Antonio de Bexar. The move followed an inspection trip by the Marquis de Rubi and the recommendation that the Spanish consolidate their forces against Plains Indian tribes, such as the Comanche and Wichita.

While Los Adaes served as the colonial capital, it marked the northeastern end of El Camino Real ("the Royal Highway") that began at the presidio of San Juan Bautista, described in the South Texas chapter of this book. One of the first drives of cattle and sheep, which were later to become such a notable part of Texas history, passed San Juan Bautista in late summer 1721 on the way to Los Adaes.

Environment: An early eighteenth-century map shows Los Adaes in a defensive position atop an east-west trending erosional remnant overlooking the Arroyo de Chacon in what is today the Pineywoods of northwestern Louisiana. The northwestern Louisiana forests represent a western portion of the Southern Pinelands, which begin in the pine barrens of New Jersey, extend south through the Atlantic states, west through the Gulf states to East Texas, and north along the Mississippi River and its tributaries. This vast forested area contains representatives of numerous biological communities typical of warm, relatively humid climates.

Los Adaes lies near the boundary between a community identified as the Southeastern Mixed Forest Province and another known as the Outer Coastal Plain Forest Province. The soils tend to be wet, acidic, and low in major plant nutrients; they range from heavy clay to gravels but tend to be sandy.

Plants. The plants are characteristic of a temperate, mixed evergreen-and-hardwood forest. Longleaf pine (*Pinus palustris*), shortleaf pine (*Pinus echinata*), and loblolly (*Pinus taeda*) are dominant pines, and typical hardwoods include oak (*Quercus* spp.), elm (*Ulmus* spp.), and magnolia (*Magnolia* spp.). Lowland areas are distinguished by frequent, intermittent ponds and lakes with stands of bald cypress (*Taxodium distichum*) draped with Spanish moss (*Tillandsia usneoides*). Grasses characteristic of the frequent open meadows include bluestems (*Andropogon* spp.), Indian grass (*Sorghastrum nutans*), and switch grass (*Panicum virgatum*).

Animals. There is a wide variety of animal life. The white-tailed deer (*Odocoileus virginianus*) is today the only large indigenous mammal. Besides the ubiquitous white-tailed deer, species characteristic of the Pineywoods include opossum (*Didelphis virginiana*), wild boar (*Sus scrofa*), gopher (*Geomys bursarius*), gray squirrel (*Sciurus carolinensis*), and American alligator (*Alligator mississipiensis*).

Archeology: One of the classic problems in archeology is that of connecting the historic with the prehistoric, the present with the past. That can be done in a general way through dating techniques, ethnographic analogy, and close comparison of various cultural characteristics. Even when dealing with well-documented historical sources, it is difficult enough to identify a specific place and connect it with a historical event. The difficulty increases as the number and reliability of historic sources become less and less. In locating and identifying a site such as Los Adaes, a major problem that must be addressed in historic archeology is the positive identification of a particular site.

Although the general location of Los Adaes had been known since a fort was established there to block French expansion into Spanish territory, its exact location was lost. The establishment of the fort followed the relocation and rebuilding of structures associated with the Mission San Miguel de Linares near the bank of Arroyo Hondo. As the following quote from one of the most respected students of the Spanish colonial period in

Texas indicates, the site was believed to be the same as the presently identified site, but conclusive evidence was lacking.

San Miguel de Linares, fifth mission established in 1716 among Adaes Indians, located near the bank of present day Arroyo Hondo, seven or eight leagues from Natchitoches and about a league from Spanish Lake. The place is identified with the site of modern Robeline, Louisiana; formal possession of this mission given to Father Margil, President of the Zacatecan friars; Alarcon welcomed by missionaries and Indians on his official tour of inspection; in 1719 the French of Louisiana made a surprise attack on this mission; deserted; its settlement protested by M. Rerenor before Aguayo without result; possession granted to Father Margil for the Zacatecan friars; ministered for a while from presidial chapel by Father Margil (Castañeda 1936:387).

Elsewhere, Castañeda provides the following information about Los Adaes: From September 1 through November 4, 1721, the Spanish built the Presidio of Los Adaes half a league beyond where the old mission had stood, near a spring of water, which flowed down a small hill. Here the presidio was stoutly built with a stockade of pointed logs two and three-quarters varas high all around it. The presidio was hexagonal in shape with three bulwarks placed on alternate corners, each protecting two sides. A garrison of one hundred men was placed in charge of the presidio which was officially named Presidio de Nuestra Señora del Pilar. Twenty-eight of these were married men and all were fully equipped with arms and horses. Six brass fieldpieces brought from Mexico were placed in the presidio and the necessary powder and balls supplied (Castañeda 1936:143).

On September 29, the Mission de San Miguel de los Adaes was officially ordered reestablished, but the mission itself was not officially reestablished at that time. In celebration of the event, feasts were held in October or early November 1721. Plays performed during the feasts were likely the first plays given in Texas. They followed by only three years the earliest known perfor-

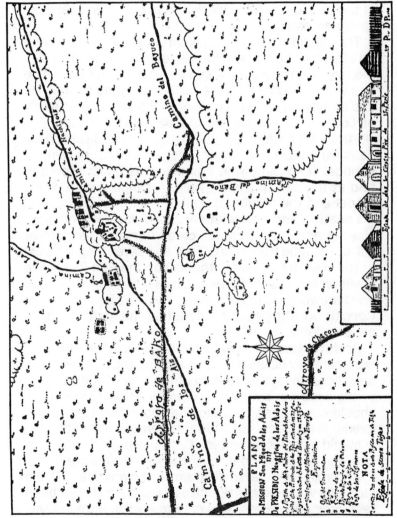

16. Los Adaes in the eighteenth century. (Map courtesy Williamson Museum, Northwestern State University, Natchitoches, Louisiana.)

mances in North America, at Williamsburg, Virginia (Castañeda 1936:143–145). An early eighteenth-century map shows that Los Adaes had grown to sizable proportions (Fig. 16). Thus, although historical sources indicate that the hill northeast of Robeline was probably the site of the presidio, until recently it had not been positively identified as such.

The solution to such a problem usually involves a careful search of historical sources to create a detailed (the more details the better) idea of where the site should be and what it should look like, including types of artifacts and architectural styles to be found there. Such a study of Los Adaes was carried out by Dr. H. F. Gregory of Northwestern State University of Louisiana. Based on exhaustive historical analysis, Gregory (1973) developed a model describing what archeologists could expect to find at the site of the presidio. A simplification of his model and the results of limited testing of it include:

Location and environment. Los Adaes was on a red clay hill, across a spring-fed creek from another, similar hill, one league from a large lake and seven leagues west of the French fort (Natchitoches) on the Red River. The environment was characterized by a mixed forest of pines and hardwoods with deer, waterfowl, and bear available. Conclusion: The popularly identified site matches those expectations.

Architectural styles. Two categories of architecture were carefully delineated, house types and stockade construction. Houses were expected to be of a distinctive wattle-daub construction known as *bousillage*. Houses should have great, overhanging roofs, two rooms with interior fireplaces, and hardware characteristic of the early to mid eighteenth century. Conclusion: Exploratory excavation revealed houses of the expected style.

According to detailed diagrams and maps (Fig. 17), the stockade was hexagonal, with wall trenches at least three feet deep and a water well constructed in Roman style. The construction was believed to be lacking in craftsmanship. Conclusion: Test excavation confirmed most of the expectations.

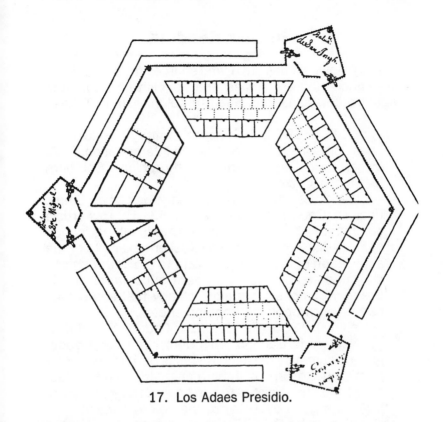

17. Los Adaes Presidio.

Small artifacts. European artifacts should include majolica (a distinctive Spanish pottery with a soft paste and a hard, shiny glazed surface) made from about 1720 to 1773, French ceramics such as faience (French pottery similar to majolica in execution) of the same period, various metal objects (specifically *ficas,* small, handcrafted metal items to ward off the evil eye), French gun flints, glass bottles, and trade beads. Indian artifacts predicted included shell-tempered pottery and trade items. Conclusion: All the items were found as predicted.

As a result of Gregory's work, the exact site of the Presidio de Nuestra Senora del Pilar de los Adaes has again been firmly identified, and the utility of historic archeology once again demonstrated.

Further Reading

The following titles are useful sources for further reading concerning Los Adaes, the Spanish occupation in western Louisiana, and Spanish colonialism in Texas.

Gregory, H. F. 1973. Eighteenth Century Caddoan Archaeology: A Study in Models and Interpretation. Ph.D. dissertation, Department of Anthropology, Southern Methodist University.

——. 1983. Los Adaes: The Archaeology of an Ethnic Enclave. *Geoscience and Man* 23:53–57. This article summarizes the methodology used in site validation at Los Adaes and is also an excellent example of the application of archeological data to the anthropological understanding of a modern subcultural group. Gregory demonstrates quite clearly that archeology can be anthropology. Recommended.

—— (editor). 1986. *The Southern Caddo: An Anthology.* New York: Garland. This book provides a good, general summary of various aspects of the Caddo from prehistoric to early historic times. Although the Caddo are mostly unrelated to Los Adaes in a direct sense, it gives a good overview of the cultural region.

Castañeda, Carlos E. 1936. The mission era: The winning of Texas, 1693–1731. *Our Catholic Heritage in Texas,* Vol. 2. Austin: Von Boeckmann-Jones.

EDWARDS PLATEAU/
HILL COUNTRY REGION

In many ways this is one of the most delightful regions of the state in which to live. Although never heavily populated by today's standards, it was the most heavily populated part of the state during the Archaic period and has been continuously occupied since. It seems people have enjoyed life here for quite some time.

The northern boundary of the region blends imperceptibly into the Panhandle-Plains and the Central Prairies. The southern and eastern boundaries are sharply delineated by the distinctive Balcones Escarpment, and the Pecos River clearly marks the western boundary (Fig. 18).

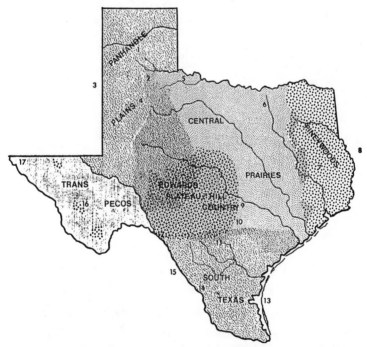

18. Edwards Plateau/Hill Country region. 9. McKinney Falls. 10. Aquarena Springs. 11. San Antonio Missions 12. Seminole Canyon.

Hundreds of interesting sites are scattered through the region, but the most important and most accessible sites lie on the interface between the high ground of the plateau and the lower prairies and plains. Technically, three of the four sites presented here lie in the Central Prairies, but they are included in this chapter based on cultural similarities, geographic similarity, and proximity to the region. The four archeological sites are McKinney Falls, Aquarena Springs, San Antonio Missions, and Seminole Canyon.

McKinney Falls State Park
7102 Scenic Loop Road
Route 2, Box 701B
Austin, Texas 78744
(512) 243-1643

General description: The park is 12 miles southeast of downtown Austin off U.S. Highway 183 on Scenic Loop Road. It consists of more than 630 acres of brushy upland and lowland areas at the confluence of Onion Creek and Williamson Creek, two major tributaries of the Colorado River basin south of Austin. The area is interesting in terms of archeology, history, and biology as well as geology. There is an interpretative center, a hike-bike trail, and a self-guided nature trail (Fig. 19). The Smith Rockshelter and the McKinney Homestead are interesting archeological features. A group meeting facility, camping, showers, and restrooms are available. The park is open until 10 P.M. weeknights and midnight Saturday. Standard state park fees are charged.

Altitude: 530 feet above mean sea level
Average annual precipitation: 32 inches
Average January minimum temperature: 41°F
Average July maximum temperature: 95°F

Standard archeological interpretation:
Site: Smith Rockshelter (41TV42; site numbers are explained in the section on Hueco Tanks)
Type of site: Rockshelter
Developmental stage: Hunting and gathering
Archeological period: Late Archaic
Dates: 1,400 years ago–recent
Archeological culture: Austin Focus, Toyah Focus
Diagnostic traits: *Scallorn* and *Perdiz* arrow points, bone and shell beads, pendants, *Leon* plain pottery

Site: McKinney Homestead (41TV289)
Type of site: Historic structures
Developmental stage: Historic

Archeological period: Historic
Dates: 1840's–1940's
Archeological culture: Historic
Diagnostic traits: Historic items

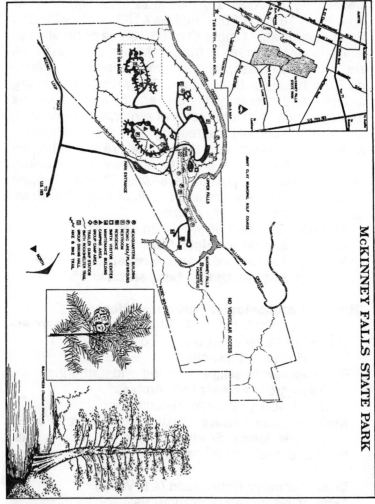

19. McKinney Falls State Park. (Map courtesy Texas Parks and
Wildlife.)

Comment: The countryside near Austin has some of the most pleasing natural features in Texas, and the climate might be ranked among the most agreeable anywhere. For geologists, the Pilot Knob area is of particular interest. Pilot Knob, a prominent topographic feature 2 miles to the southeast of the park interpretive center, is the remnant of a volcano that erupted from the floor of a shallow sea during the Late Cretaceous, 80 million years ago. Eventually, the volcanic rock formed an island, and a sandy beach developed around it. The modern exposure of this sandy beach is represented by the stone of the waterfalls and the roof of the Smith Rockshelter.

Environment: McKinney Falls is situated in a marginal area on the border between two major natural areas, the Edwards Plateau/Hill Country and the North Central Prairies. Specifically, the site is on the prairie, but the Balcones Escarpment, that abrupt indicator of the Hill Country margin, lies only a short distance upstream. As a consequence, McKinney Falls has a distinct Hill Country bias. In technical terms, the locale of the park is ecotonal between the two areas.

Plants. The upland plant community is dominated by trees such as mesquite (*Prosopis glandulosa*), escarpment live oak (*Quercus fusiformis*), and juniper (*Juniperus ashei*), and smaller upland plants include yucca (*Yucca* spp.), buffalo grass (*Buchloë dactyloides*), and little bluestem (*Schizachyrium scoparium*).

Vegetation along Onion Creek includes trees such as bald cypress (*Taxodium distichum*), willows (*Salix* spp.), and pecan (*Carya illinoensis*). Poison ivy (*Rhus toxicodendron*), mustang grape (*Vitis mustangensis*), and mesquite grass (*Panicum obtusum*) are characteristic small species.

Animals. Although buffalo (*Bison bison*), gray wolf (*Canis lupus*), and black bear (*Ursus americanus*) were once common species in this part of Texas, they are no longer found here. Common native animals today include white-tailed deer (*Odocoileus virginianus*), opossum (*Didelphis virginiana*), armadillo (*Dasypus novemcinctus*), and raccoon (*Procyon lotor*). The park is known for a great variety of birds, and boat-tailed grackle (*Cassidix mexicanus*), cedar waxwing (*Bombycilla cedrorum*), chimney swift (*Chaetura pelagica*), turkey (*Meleagris gallopavo*), and Mexican eagle (*Caracara cheriway*) are typical.

Archeology: The most accessible archeological sites at McKinney Falls involve various aspects of the McKinney Homestead and the Smith Rockshelter. This section highlights a particularly useful but seldom attempted type of archeology, experimental archeology, as it was employed at the McKinney Homestead. The stratigraphy at Smith Rockshelter is also outlined.

Experimental Archeology at McKinney Homestead
    Experimentation is a scientific method that has long been used in archeology to test concepts about how things were used, what is good to eat, how stone tools could have been made, and so on. Within the past two decades or so, it has become a major area of specialization within the field. The annual summer field school of the Texas Archeological Society, held in 1974 at McKinney Falls, was designed as an exercise in experimental archeology (McEachern and Ralph 1980, 1981).
    Initially, field school participants were assigned to one of five work units, each of which represented a particular experiment and a specifically stated research plan. The five experiments and their results are as follows:
    1. The first experiment was designed to determine the value of proton magnetometers, metal detectors, pH testing, and phosphate sampling as tools in archeological prospecting. To test their effectiveness, one grid system was established near the McKinney house and another was established near the old mill ruins. A proton magnetometer survey and a metal detector survey were then independently made on each of the gridded areas, and soil samples were systematically collected and analyzed. When appropriate maps were drawn and compared, it was obvious that the metal detectors and the phosphate testing were the most useful in this situation. It was con-

cluded that all the techniques hold promise, but interpreting magnetometer readings requires quite a bit of expertise, and pH testing is subject to too many variables to be useful in sites of this type.

2. The second experiment was intended as a straightforward excavation of the McKinney house, guided by a detailed list of expectations developed from historical sources. Results were about as expected: excavations in the east room of the house and in two trenches leading north and east from the east room turned up data concerning architecture as well as metal, bottle glass, and ceramic artifacts. Excavation of the east ditch provided clear examples of the use of lists of expectations, sometimes called predictive models, in archeological investigation. Although most of the excavation in the east ditch produced expected results, the results from unit E1 (near the house) and units E4 and E5 (both some distance from the house) were drastically different from what had been predicted. Dramatic, unexpected results are called anomalies; they are useful since they point out areas that demand explanation. In this case unit E1, near the front of the house and almost devoid of artifacts, was interpreted as part of the ground under the front porch. Units E4 and E5, which had an unexpectedly large number of artifacts, were interpreted as part of a rumored trash dump.

3. This experiment was designed to provide information on the population of small animals in the area at the time the cistern provided a well-defined trap for them. A combination of a large number of artifacts, remains of small animals, and the stratigraphic characteristics of deposits were found in the cistern fill. The evidence (artifacts such as bottles dated just after the turn of the century) indicated that the cistern began being filled about 1900 and seemed to stop in the mid-thirties. During that period opossums, rabbits, snakes, various rodents, lizards, and frogs were among the animals trapped in the cistern. It was concluded that the results of the cistern experiment were much better than expected.

4. The fourth experiment involved excavation of the

old mill ruins following essentially the same, traditional plan used in excavations at the house. Goals were to identify the location of the mill walls and determine the type of mill and the direction of the outlet tunnel. The mill excavations went as expected and produced the desired results. One of the most exciting events of the dig was the unexpected discovery of the mill blades (turbine)— the turbine turned out to be a design that provided important information about millwrighting technology in the mid-nineteenth century.

5. The fifth experiment was developed after the original agenda had been completed. An ongoing project at McKinney Falls, it is an experimental time capsule that involves a second cistern. Cistern 2, at the time of discovery, had been filled to about four meters from the surface with material assumed to be similar to the fill in cistern 1. The deposit was sealed off with sterile fill, and the remaining wall exposure was painted to mark the long-term archeological experiment. A documented list of modern artifacts "representing a complete array of material types currently in use" were then buried in stratigraphic alternation with sterile dirt to the top of the cistern. By 2024, the deposit will be fifty years old and eligible for inclusion in the National Register of Historic Places. The project simultaneously preserves part of the original deposit in the cistern for future research, begins a project for studying the effects of time on various modern artifacts, provides a controlled means for studying intrasite change, and comprises a time capsule of artifacts from the 1974 field school of the Texas Archeological Society.

All in all, the work done by the 1974 field school might well serve as a model for all such field schools. It provided an excellent opportunity for participants to learn various aspects of modern archeology in an efficient, well-planned, and satisfying way. The McKinney Homestead project is public archeology at its best.

Stratigraphic Sequence at Smith Rockshelter
The Smith Rockshelter, in a limestone bluff overlook-

ing Onion Creek, is a major stopping point in the Smith Rockshelter Nature Trail at McKinney Falls State Park. The term "rockshelter" is discussed at the end of this chapter in the Seminole Canyon section. The present section simply summarizes some of the early work done here.

From the perspective of the maturation of archeology in the state, this work is an excellent example of archeological work and interpretation as it was practiced in Texas in the fifties. Archeology then was done in a typological mode, most characterized by the just-published book *An Introductory Handbook of Texas Archeology* (Suhm, Krieger, and Jelks 1954). Dee Ann Suhm, the principal author of this now-classic publication in Texas archeology, was also the driving force behind the excavation, analysis, and reporting of Smith Rockshelter and, as we might say today, was on a roll. Some of the things done then would no longer be done now, other things would be done differently, and things now considered important were omitted then, but the excavation, analysis, and reporting were the state of the art in Texas in the fifties and, not so incidentally, have withstood the test of time pretty well.

The first controlled, systematic excavations at Smith Rockshelter were carried out on weekends from early October 1954 until August 1955, by student volunteers from the University of Texas (Suhm 1957). During that initial effort an area of 1,125 square feet of the floor was excavated in 5-foot-square units. Approximately half the units were dug to bedrock. The excavations revealed a clear stratigraphic alternation of occupational layers with sterile layers. Results of that study and other investigations are interpreted here.

When the site was dug, eleven layers were recognized in stratigraphic profile. Upon analysis, it was concluded that the eleven layers represented three distinct occupational periods.

Occupational period 1. This represents the earliest occupation at the site and is found only in layer 1, bedrock to about 6 feet below the surface. It is representative of the Late Archaic Stage and is dated approximately 1,400–1,250 years ago. The occupation was considered to be a local representation of a larger social unit, the Uvalde Focus, which itself was thought to be part of the Edwards Plateau Aspect, a major subdivision of the Archaic Stage in Texas. Artifact types considered diagnostic of the Uvalde Focus include *Darl, Ensor,* and *Edgewood* dart point types.

Occupational period 2. This period, represented in the bulk of the deposit in Smith Rockshelter, is found in the upper portions of layer 1 and extends through layer 9, about 6 feet to 1 foot below the surface of the deposit in the shelter. It was thought to represent a social unit called the Austin Focus (at that time a part of the Late Prehistoric), about 1,250–650 years ago. Typical artifacts of the Austin Focus include point types such as *Scallorn* and *Granbury,* which represent the earliest use of arrows in this part of Texas. The difference between the Austin Focus and the earlier Uvalde Focus is marked by the shift from use of the spearthrower (*atl-atl*) in the Uvalde Focus to the earliest use of the bow and arrow in the Austin Focus.

From the point of view of fieldwork, the excavation of these levels typically requires the greatest physical and psychological effort of the enterprise. Often there are major obstacles such as massive rocks, slumping walls, and waning enthusiasms that must be overcome if the dig is to proceed through this phase of fieldwork.

Occupational period 3. Evidence of this period—the final prehistoric occupation known at Smith Rockshelter—is confined to the uppermost level, layer 11, the upper 10 inches of the deposit. The surface as it appears today is similar to the way it appeared at the time of this occupation, called the Toyah Focus, 650–200 years ago. The Toyah Focus is distinguished from the earlier Austin Focus by the presence of *Perdiz* and *Cliffton* arrowpoint types and, perhaps more important, the appearance of *Leon* plain, the earliest known pottery in this part of Texas.

Further Reading

The reader is reminded that descriptions of artifact types may be found in Suhm, Krieger, and Jelks (1954), Suhm and Jelks (1962), and Turner and Hester (1985).

McEachern, M., and R. W. Ralph. 1980. Archeological investigations at the Thomas F. McKinney homestead, Travis County, Texas: An experiment in historic archeology, part I. *Bulletin of the Texas Archeological Society* 51:5–208.

———. 1981. Archeological investigations at the Thomas F. McKinney homestead, Travis County, Texas: An experiment in historical archeology, part II. *Bulletin of the Texas Archeological Society* 52:5–63. These publications offer a thorough review of the work done by the Texas Archeological Society field school and include a number of detailed appendices dealing with various aspects of the work at McKinney Falls. Recommended.

Suhm, Dee Ann. 1957. Excavations at the Smith Rockshelter, Travis County, Texas. *Texas Journal of Science* 9(1):26–58. An excellent example of Texas archeology in the mid fifties, this is a basic reference in Central Texas archeology.

Suhm, Dee Ann, and Edward B. Jelks (editors). 1962. *Handbook of Texas Archeology: Type Descriptions.* Austin: Texas Archeological Society, Special Publication No. 1, and Texas Memorial Museum, Bulletin No. 4.

Suhm, Dee Ann, Alex D. Krieger, and Edward B. Jelks. 1954. *An Introductory Handbook of Texas Archeology.* Bulletin of the Texas Archeological Society, Vol. 25.

Turner, Ellen Sue, and Thomas R. Hester. 1985. *A Field Guide to Stone Artifacts of Texas Indians.* Austin: Texas Monthly Press.

Aquarena Springs
Loop 82
San Marcos, Texas
(512) 392-2481

General description: The entrance to Aquarena Springs is at the intersection of Old Highway 81 and Loop 82 northeast of Southwest Texas State University in San Marcos. Aquarena Springs is operated as a private, commercial venture that features various amusements centering around Spring Lake, an artificial pond created in the late nineteenth century by damming the flow from the springs. Glass-bottomed boats take visitors over the springs where "sand boils" caused by active spring flow can be observed clearly. Schools of large fish, other animals (such as salamanders, turtles, and snakes), and a great variety of plant species make up a unique biology plainly visible through the bottom of the boats. Also to be seen, but not visited, is an open campsite that was occupied by Paleoindian and Archaic peoples over several thousand years.

Altitude: 580 feet above mean sea level
Average annual precipitation: 34 inches
Average January minimum temperature: 40°F
Average July maximum temperature: 96°F

Standard archeological interpretation:
Site: 41HY147 (site numbers are explained in the section on Hueco Tanks)
Type of site: Now-submerged open camp
Developmental stage: Hunting and gathering
Archeological period: Paleoindian; Archaic
Dates: 8000 B.C.–A.D. 1600
Archeological culture: Various
Diagnostic traits: *Clovis, Plainview, Angostura* points; mastodon, mammoth, and bison bones

Comment: Forming a lovely, crystal-clear lake at the base of the impressive Balcones Escarpment, Aquarena

Springs is surely one of the most naturally beautiful places in the state. Although a Disneyland-like frenzy has enveloped the place in the last several decades, enough natural beauty remains to charge the spirit. It is still possible to experience the serenity and promise this site has offered to human psyches since people were first attracted here more than 11,000 years ago. A visit to this site provides an excellent opportunity to explore the geology and biology of one of Texas' famed artesian springs as well as the chance to experience the environment in which some of the state's most innovative archeology has been under way.

After a visit to Aquarena Springs, Pepper's restaurant in San Marcos is a convenient place to stop and appreciate the volume of flow from the springs as the water thunders over the waterfall from Spring Lake.

Environment: Aquarena Springs offers a good opportunity to study several aspects of the natural history of the area and how human activity is tied to changes in that natural history. This section will emphasize the geography of the springs in this region and some residents of the plant and animal communities.

The Balcones Escarpment and Its Springs
San Marcos, like Del Rio, San Antonio, New Braunfels, and Austin, is a modern Texas city founded at the edge of the Balcones Escarpment. Each of those cities represents the modern expression of a cultural presence that has been persistent at these sites since the earliest human occupation of the area more than 10,000 years ago. Each city has its own manifestation of a common reason for these settlements—water. In the semiarid environment of this part of Texas, the ready availability of abundant fresh water was a determining factor in the establishment of cities. In that respect, the oldest Texas cities are similar to the oldest cities throughout the world. Cities are established where there is an abundance of water.

The five cities, each located at the source of one of

the five largest artesian springs in Texas, are listed in order of size of spring as measured by flow: New Braunfels at Comal Springs, Comal County; San Marcos at Aquarena Springs, Hays County; Del Rio at San Felipe Springs, Val Verde County (Goodenough Springs, also in Val Verde County, was the third largest in Texas but is now covered by the waters of Amistad Reservoir), Austin at Barton Springs, Travis County; and San Antonio at San Antonio Springs, Bexar County. In addition to the major springs, there are numerous smaller springs in the immediate area of each, so the combined downstream flow is greater than that from the largest alone. In San Antonio, for example, the flow from San Pedro Springs and Olmos Springs joins that of San Antonio Springs to provide a substantial flow in the San Antonio River in the vicinity of the San Antonio missions.

The cities are situated on the Balcones Fault Zone and are at or near the most conspicuous feature of that geologic phenomenon, the Balcones Escarpment. An escarpment is a geographic feature that marks the edge between two distinctly different surfaces. Thus, the Balcones Escarpment marks the southern and southeastern edge of the Edwards Plateau, which is about 800 feet higher than the Gulf Coastal Plain where the springs emerge. The escarpment looms over a traveler like a massive balcony, hence the name "Balcones." It extends from the vicinity of Del Rio eastward to San Antonio, then northeastward to San Marcos, Austin, and Georgetown, and finally is lost in the hills west of Waco. It was formed about 17 million years ago when the Edwards Plateau rose several hundred feet higher than the coastal plain, creating the balconylike range along the Balcones Fault Zone.

Rain falling on the Edwards Plateau flows through cracks in the underlying limestone into a vast underground reservoir known as the Edwards Aquifer. The aquifer consists of a vast network of caves, sinkholes, cracks, and tunnels in the Edwards limestone formation that provides the foundation for the Edwards Plateau. Limestone is a relatively soluble rock and becomes honeycombed by water erosion. Numerous caves such as Longhorn Caverns, Cave Without a Name, Innerspace Caverns, Caverns of Sonora, and Cascade Caverns give the casual visitor a chance to see parts of the aquifer. There are many other opportunities open to the more adventurous.

Springs such as the ones under discussion occur where the underground water is forced to the surface. The water in the Edwards Aquifer flows from higher elevations in the northwest toward lower elevations in the southeast. At the Balcones Fault Zone, the water flowing through the aquifer is forced to the surface when it comes into contact with harder rock such as shale. In a sense the springs act as a spillway for the aquifer. As long as the reservoir is full, water overflows, and the springs are active. But when the water level of the aquifer drops, the flow diminishes and can stop altogether.

The following is a synopsis of characteristics of Texas' five largest springs. The data are derived in large part from the *Texas Almanac* (1987) and Brune (1981).

Comal Springs. The major active sources of this, the largest springs in Texas, are easily visited at Landa Park, New Braunfels. The annual flow averages well over 2,000 gallons per second. The maximum flow was measured on October 16, 1973, at about 3,700 gallons per second. Comal Springs stopped flowing from June 13 through November 3, 1953, near the end of a great drought, illustrating the need for consistent recharging of the aquifer to maintain the springs' flow. The main recharge watershed for Comal Springs lies about 60 miles northwest of New Braunfels. It is estimated that water from a heavy rain on the watershed takes one or two months to reach Comal Springs.

Aquarena Springs. Second largest in Texas, these springs were known as San Marcos Springs until recently. Located in San Marcos, they are easy to visit. Maximum recorded flow was about 2,200 gallons per second on June 12, 1975; minimum flow was 320 gallons per second on August 15, 1956. Annual flow averages about 1,000 gallons per second. More than half the water issuing from Aquarena Springs is thought to be overflow from the same sources that feed Comal Springs. The remainder seems to come from a recharge area where streams such as the Blanco and Guadalupe rivers cross the Balcones Fault Zone.

San Felipe Springs. The westernmost of the five springs, San Felipe, arises in the southeastern part of Del Rio. Water from the springs supplies the city and Laughlin Air Force Base. The maximum flow was recorded at 1,200 gallons per second on July 23, 1976; minimum flow was about 210 gallons per second on July 29, 1964. The recharge area is thought to be about 60 miles north and east in the vicinity of Sonora, Sheffield, and Eldorado.

Barton Springs. This may be the best-known springs in Texas. Long a popular point of relaxation for students at the University of Texas, the Barton Springs swimming area is nestled in a fold of the Balcones Escarpment at Zilker Park, Austin. The flow from Barton Springs has varied from a high of approximately 2,200 gallons per second in 1941 to a low of about 70 gallons per second in 1956. The flow rate, averaged over an 80-year period, is about 350 gallons per second.

San Antonio Springs. Until the submergence in 1968 of third-ranked Goodenough Springs in Val Verde County, San Antonio Springs was listed as sixth in volume of flow, but now it is ranked fifth. As mentioned elsewhere in this book, San Antonio Springs supplies a substantial part of the flow of the San Antonio River. It and other springs in the area, such as San Pedro Springs and Olmos Springs, have been important factors in the development of the modern city of San Antonio. Control of the waters and protection of the aquifer from which they issue is currently a matter of political significance there—as, I believe, it should be wherever people have become dependent on underground water. Such water is a variable and fragile resource.

San Antonio Springs is on both public and private property in northcentral San Antonio. Maximum recorded rate of flow was almost 1,500 gallons per second in 1920, but the flow has stopped for extended periods on several occasions. The rate of discharge averaged over several years has been about 350 gallons per second. The recharge area lies 20 to 60 miles to the west and northwest of downtown San Antonio where rivers such as the Medina, Sabinal, and Frio and creeks such as the Leon and Hondo cross the Balcones Fault Zone.

Plant and Animal Communities at Aquarena Springs
The site of the Aquarena Springs lies, as do similarly situated sites at McKinney Falls and the San Antonio Missions, upon the Gulf Coastal Plain, but it is adjacent to the Hill Country/Edwards Plateau region. Consequently, the biological mix here is derived from both regions.

The plant and animal communities are made further complicated, and interesting, by the habitat offered by the springs themselves. The presence of the springs constitutes a conservative force in the local environment. The availability of a constant and reliable source of water is obviously a stabilizing force, but other factors associated with the springs are not so obvious. For example, the fairly constant temperature of the water at about 72° Fahrenheit means that winters are warmer and summers milder in the immediate vicinity of the springs. Also, evaporation from the springs raises the humidity of the immediate area providing environmental niches for species not ordinarily found in the surrounding natural regions. All in all, this site and others like it have provided attractive places for human habitation for more than 11,000 years—as long as there have been people in the area.

Plants. Trees include mesquite (*Prosopis glandulosa*), huisache (*Acacia farnesiana*), bald cypress (*Taxodium distichum*), willow (*Salix* spp.), juniper (*Juniperus ashei*), escarpment live oak (*Quercus fusiformis*), hackberry (*Celtis reticulata*), Texas persimmon (*Diospyros texana*), and Mexican plum (*Prunus mexicana*). Agarita (*Berberis trifoliolata*), mustang grape (*Vitis mustangensis*), yucca (*Yucca* spp.), poison ivy (*Rhus toxicodendron*), and prickly pear (*Opuntia lindheimeri*) are characteristic mid-size species, and sunflower (*Helianthus* spp.), Texas bluebonnet

(*Lupinus texensis*), buffalo grass (*Buchloë dactyloides*), and little bluestem (*Schizachyrium scoparium*) are conspicuous flowers and grasses. Texas wild rice (*Zizania texana*) is one of several endemic species that are found in marshes, ponds, and lakes associated with the springs but are not characteristic of either the Edwards Plateau or this part of the coastal plain.

Animals. Native animals include mammals such as white-tailed deer (*Odocoileus virginianus*), opossum (*Didelphis virginiana*), armadillo (*Dasypus novemcinctus*), and raccoon (*Procyon lotor*). Gray wolf (*Canis lupus*) and black bear (*Ursus americanus*), once common species in historic times, are no longer found here. Recent archeological work at Aquarena Springs has indicated that mammoth (*Parelphas columbi*) and other Ice Age species were not only in the area but were also hunted by early human populations. Unique aquatic forms include a dwarf salamander (*Eurycea nana*) and a giant freshwater shrimp (*Macrobrachium carcinus*).

Archeology: Beginning in 1978, a most innovative series of excavations has been performed at Aquarena Springs, under the persistent direction of Dr. Joel L. Shiner, of the Department of Anthropology at Southern Methodist University. That work, innovative both in method and result, is the subject of discussion here.

Aquarena Springs, San Antonio Springs, Comal Springs, and the other artesian springs discussed above have long been the central feature of local environments. They have attracted and maintained distinctive communities wherever they have emerged. It has been well known for some time that human occupation is characteristic of these communities, and archeological sites are always found in the immediate vicinity of the springs.

The free flow of the Aquarena Springs was blocked in the late nineteenth century by construction of a dam about 300 yards downstream from the largest spring. The springs and adjacent stream banks were covered by about 16 feet of water, which forms the lake that visitors see today. The innovative methodology at Aquarena Springs has centered upon the special circumstances of excavation of an underwater site. Although underwater archeology has been more and more widely practiced in the last several decades, it is still unusual, and the opportunity to see a site where underwater excavation has been carried out is rare.

Underwater archeology, properly conducted, has all the requirements of dryland excavation but carries its own set of problems and conveniences. The always present problem of excavation with systematic control is made more difficult by the underwater environment. Mapping, gridding, and the specific problem of dirt moving all have new dimensions under the water. Added to those technical problems are logistical problems of communication and surface support systems, along with the difficulties of scuba and other forms of diving.

As excavation at the springs proceeded, three distinct strata were determined (Shiner 1983). The uppermost stratum, characterized by a gray clay matrix 10 inches thick, was found to have artifacts associated with an archeological unit sometimes designated the Edwards Plateau Aspect. Specifically, barbed and shouldered projectile points of various Archaic types were reported. The middle stratum consists mostly of a red sand deposit about 6 inches thick and contains a mixture of artifact types found in each of the other strata. The lowest reported stratum is composed of a red clay matrix a little more than a foot thick. It was found to contain material with the most interesting implications. This material, Paleoindian projectile point types including *Clovis, Plainview,* and *Angostura* and remains of such Ice Age animals as mastodon, mammoth, and bison, was interpreted as representing "an almost sedentary hunting and gathering existence" (Shiner 1983:2). That interpretation was reinforced by analysis of collections made at similar sites in Central Texas. It now appears that contrary to previous interpretations, Paleoindian hunters and gatherers were not migratory big-game hunters but, where possible, adopted a much more sedentary existence. That is, the relatively permanent base-camp pattern of subsistence often associated with the arrival of Archaic period hunters and gatherers had been adopted by much earlier Paleoindian groups where local circumstances permitted.

Further Reading

Brune, G. 1981. *Springs of Texas,* Vol. 1. Fort Worth: Branch-Smith. This is the most comprehensive single source available on the subject of Texas springs, containing discussions of springs in general, their history, physical setting, human relations with springs, and laws and springs. The bulk of the book describes and gives the location of specific springs by county. All but 77 Texas counties are represented.

Shiner, Joel L. 1983. Large springs and early American Indians. *Plains Anthropologist* 28(99):1–7. This brief article describes Shiner's early work at Aquarena Springs and outlines the development of his argument that Paleoindians established a more-or-less permanent residence at sites such as this in Central Texas.

The Alamo
Alamo Plaza
San Antonio, Texas 78201
(512) 222-1693

San Antonio Missions National Historical Park
The Superintendent
727 E. Durango Boulevard
San Antonio, Texas 78206
(512) 229-5701

Mission San José
Mission Road at Roosevelt Avenue
2202 Roosevelt Avenue
San Antonio, Texas 78210
(512) 229-4770

Mission San Francisco de la Espada
10040 Espada Road
San Antonio, Texas
(512) 627-2021

Mission Concepción
807 Mission Road
San Antonio, Texas
(512) 229-5732

Mission San Juan Capistrano
Graf Road at Ashley Road
9001 Graf Road
San Antonio, Texas
(512) 229-5734

Espada Aqueduct
9044 Espada Road
San Antonio, Texas

General description: The Alamo and the five sites of the San Antonio Missions National Historical Park are distributed along the San Antonio River in San Antonio, Texas. The church of the Mission San Antonio de Valero (the Alamo) is in the center of downtown San Antonio, where it forms the hub of the most visited spot in Texas. A museum, shop, and lovely gardens are enclosed by impressive stone walls that may resemble the original walls, but then again, they may not. Open Monday through Saturday from 9:30 A.M. to 5 P.M., Sunday from 10 A.M. to 5:30 P.M. Tours available for groups. No charge, but donations are accepted.

The San Antonio Missions National Historical Park was authorized on November 10, 1978, and is exceptional in several ways. A total of 475 acres is divided among several discrete units, the churches at each of the missions continue to be used for Catholic services and other parish activities, and the hours of operation change to accommodate Daylight Saving Time. The four missions in the park, Mission Concepción, Mission San José, Mission San Juan, and Mission Espada, are open daily from 8 A.M. to 5 P.M. (Central Standard Time) and from 9 A.M. to 6 P.M. (Daylight Saving Time) and at other times for church activities. The fifth unit in the park, the Espada Aqueduct, is accessible at all hours. Most locations have small interpretive centers, guides, or self-guided trails. There is a small admission fee at each mission or a slightly larger fee for a pass to all four missions.

Altitude: 550–650 feet above mean sea level
Average annual precipitation: 28 inches
Average January minimum temperature: 42°F
Average July maximum temperature: 94°F
Standard archeological interpretation:
Site: San Antonio missions
Type of site: Special-purpose, occupational, village
Developmental stage: Historic
Archeological period: Historic
Dates: 1719–present
Archeological culture: Spanish colonial, Mexican
Diagnostic traits: Historic artifacts

Comment: A tremendous mythology surrounds Spanish mission sites wherever they occur in North America, and the San Antonio sites are no exception. Romantic sagas have prevailed over revisionist attempts to such an extent that the data offered by historians and archeologists have seldom been accepted unless they reinforce or flesh out a particular romantic account. That situation has prevailed in San Antonio and is especially apparent in the case of the Alamo, a site that has the emotional impact of a holy place. The result is quite simply that there is no standard archeological interpretation apart from standard historical interpretations.

The sites are presented here as a unit because they represent a unit of time and culture—Spanish religious and economic colonialism—that was the major force of early San Antonio history, a force that was responsible for many of the most distinctive characteristics of this beautiful Texas city.

The Alamo is well known, but the Missions National Historical Park is relatively new and undiscovered by the general public. Established in 1978 to help preserve remnants of the Spanish colonial period in the United States and to make them more accessible to the general public, it consists of five discrete units scattered along the San Antonio River south of the Alamo (Fig. 20). There are four clusters of mission buildings—Mission Concepción, Mission San José, Mission San Juan, and Mission Espada—and the graceful remnants of a once-extensive irrigation system, the Espada Aqueduct.

The missions still are used for regular church activities as well as historical and archeological purposes. This section includes a location map of all the sites, an outline of the history of the missions, and an example of archeological work at some of them.

Environment: San Antonio, one of those modern Texas cities established at the edge of the Balcones Escarpment, today lies partly on the Edwards Plateau, straddles the escarpment, and sprawls onto the Gulf Coastal Plain. It is favorably situated for exploitation of three of the

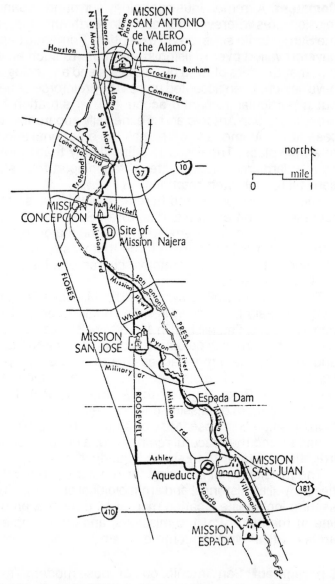

20. San Antonio Missions National Historic Park. (Map courtesy National Park Service.)

major natural and cultural areas described earlier in this book. To the north and west lies the broken topography of the Edwards Plateau/Hill Country, the vast coastal plain stretches south to the Gulf of Mexico, and most of the city itself sits near the end of a narrow southern belt of the North Central Prairies at the headwaters of the spring-fed San Antonio River, a water source that has been attractive to human populations since earliest prehistoric times. (See the preceding section on Aquarena Springs for a discussion of early prehistoric occupation at a similar site.)

The Balcones Escarpment (a topographic feature that extends eastward from the vicinity of Del Rio until it reaches San Antonio, where it arches toward the northeast through San Marcos and Austin) was formed about 17 million years ago when the Edwards Plateau rose several hundred feet higher than the Gulf Coastal Plain and thus formed a balconylike range along the Balcones Fault Zone. Rain falling on the Edwards Plateau flows through cracks in the underlying limestone into a vast underground reservoir known as the Edwards Aquifer. The San Antonio River receives most of its water from constantly flowing springs that issue from the aquifer. The flow of the springs has been diminishing as modern water use has dramatically increased. When visiting the sites described below, remember that the flow of the river was more abundant in the past than it is today.

As could be expected, the plant and animal communities reflect the meeting of three natural zones here. In addition, the special habitat afforded by the San Antonio River is a major factor in the local biology. The flora and fauna therefore represent a mixture of species characteristic of the Edwards Plateau/Hill Country, the North Central Prairies, the South Texas Plains, and a few relict species.

Plants. Trees include mesquite (*Prosopis glandulosa*), huisache (*Acacia farnesiana*), bald cypress (*Taxodium distichum*), willow (*Salix* spp.), juniper (*Juniperus ashei*), escarpment live oak (*Quercus fusiformis*), hackberry (*Celtis reticulata*), Texas persimmon (*Diospyros texana*), and

Mexican plum (*Prunus mexicana*). Agarita (*Berberis trifoliolata*), mustang grape (*Vitis mustangensis*), yucca (*Yucca* spp.), poison ivy (*Rhus toxicodendron*), and prickly pear (*Opuntia lindheimeri*) are characteristic mid-size species, and sunflower (*Helianthus* spp.), Texas bluebonnet (*Lupinus texensis*), buffalo grass (*Buchloë dactyloides*), and little bluestem (*Schizachyrium scoparium*) are conspicuous flowers and grasses.

Animals. Native animals include white-tailed deer (*Odocoileus virginianus*), opossum (*Didelphis virginiana*), armadillo (*Dasypus novemcinctus*), and raccoon (*Procyon lotor*) as characteristic modern species. Buffalo (*Bison bison*), gray wolf (*Canis lupus*), and black bear (*Ursus americanus*), once common species in the area, are no longer found here.

Archeology: Since so much literature is already available concerning the history of San Antonio and the missions, this section presents only a bare outline of historical events. (The reader is referred to other sources, listed at the end of this section, for more information.) The historical archeology of the various sites is considered in only slightly more detail; indeed, the archeology included here represents only a tiny fraction of that available. A tremendous amount of archeology has been done in San Antonio, especially in the last fifteen years, and the city is far ahead of others in this regard, but it is important to note that the work has just begun in this, the historically richest of all Texas cities.

Archeology at the Alamo

Three of the major functions of historical archeology—interpretation, verification, and discovery—are illustrated by recent work in the vicinity of the Alamo.

Interpretation adds new information to the historical record. For example, bones recovered at a site might add to the interpretation of the diet of the people at the site in a more specific sense than is usually possible with historic sources alone.

Verification is one of the strongest (and often most controversial) aspects of historical archeology. It uses archeological data to test historical "truths." If, for example, historical sources indicate a well at a specific location, but digging fails to find evidence of a well, then the historical account is refuted. If, on the other hand, archeological evidence of a well is found at the expected location, then the historical sources are archeologically verified. It is when the archeological evidence refutes the historical accounts that archeologists sometimes find themselves in hot water.

Discovery is one of the most exciting (and romantic) of archeological activities. Discovery overlaps the processes of verification and interpretation of historical documentation, but in its most exciting form, it adds something to the archeological knowledge that was not previously suggested by other sources. The cockroaches found on the wrecked Spanish ships off Padre Island offer a simple but interesting instance of discovery.

One of the problems in understanding the Alamo is that the modern site contains only a small part of the old mission grounds. Streets, office buildings, hotels, stores, and plaza pavements have infringed on the old structures so that it is hard to imagine, for example, what the place looked like on that morning in March 1836, when the Mexican army began its final assault. Three of the many archeological excavations at the Alamo during the last several years allow us to envision more dramatically the distances and spaces involved. One excavation revealed part of the western wall, another precisely located a Mexican army gun battery, and the third and most recent rediscovered the precise location of the main entrance to the mission compound.

Wall excavation. Excavations in 1980 revealed long-buried remains of portions of the outer, western wall of the enclosed compound. This wall, nearest the river, faced the main civilian settlement at San Antonio. It was more than a vara (a Spanish unit measuring not quite three feet) thick. Along the interior of the wall, facing the entrance to the chapel (the Alamo), was a row of Indian dwellings, similar to the replicas that can be seen today at Mission San José. Excavation of the dwelling sites revealed hearths, charred corncobs, and the bones of wild and domestic animals such as cows, goats, and deer.

An excavated portion of the western wall is displayed near the entrance to the Riverwalk, about 300 feet across Alamo Plaza from the front entrance to the Alamo. Standing there, a visitor can imagine the distances involved and get a better idea of what the defenders had to defend. There was a lot of space inside those walls! Excavation was proceeding at the main entrance to the Alamo, at the southwestern corner of the compound, as this was being written.

La Villita earthworks excavation (Fig. 21). More than 1,300 hours of work in late February and early March 1985 revealed the first archeological evidence of the Mexican side of the siege of the Alamo (Labadie 1986). This dig, near the intersection of Nueva and South Alamo streets, revealed a hand-dug, L-shaped ditch, measuring about 38 feet in length and about 7 feet below the original ground level, that was interpreted as a military earthwork, possibly an artillery battery position during the siege of the Alamo. Artifacts found in the course of excavation included English Brown Bess musket parts, English sword blades and a sword guard, bayonets, buttons, horseshoes, a four-rein bit, a Mexican-style saddle stirrup, and other articles of cavalry tack. Those artifacts, along with numerous gunflints, musket balls, and cannonballs, when compared with the few available accounts of the siege, reinforced the interpretation that this discovery was, in fact, a gun battery of the Mexican army.

A careful reading of an eyewitness account (Peña 1975) suggests that the inhabitants of this position, the men who dug the trench and warmed themselves in it on the cold night of February 23, 1836, were from San Luis Potosí. Today a visitor can stand at the southwest corner of Nueva and South Alamo streets and, facing north, obtain a better sense of what the well-defended Alamo looked like to cold, weary soldiers camped 600 yards south of the main entrance.

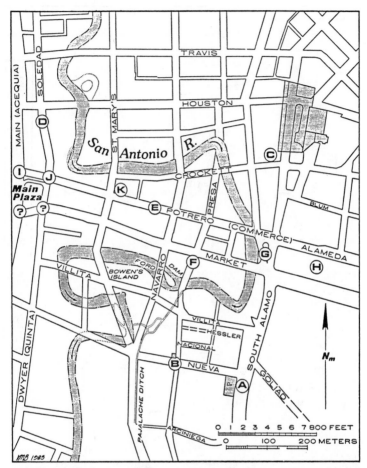

21. Battlement locations at the siege of the Alamo. Site A, La Villita earthworks. Site C, southwest corner of Alamo compound. (Map courtesy the Center for Archeological Research, University of Texas at San Antonio.)

Archeology at Mission Concepción

One of the most recent of several seasons of controlled archeological excavations at Mission Concepción was carried out in the fall of 1986 by a crew from the Center

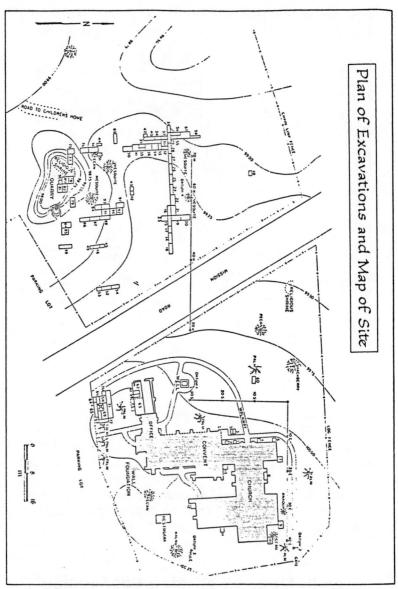

22. Mission Concepción. (Map courtesy Texas Historical Commission.)

for Archeological Research of the University of Texas at San Antonio (A. A. Fox 1988). The primary purpose of the excavations was to help solve a specific problem. The problem, investigation, and recommended solution represent a succinct example of applied archeology at its best.

The problem. A low area between the sacristy and the convent (Fig. 22) was intermittently flooded by the infrequent but severe thunderstorms characteristic of this area of Texas. Sometimes the water accumulated so rapidly that it flooded into the convent itself. Damage caused by the backed-up floodwaters was increasing, so it was decided to install a drainpipe. The problem was to plan an affordable route for the pipe that would cause the least damage to buried remains at the mission site.

The investigation. Previous work had indicated that portions of buried walls and other buried resources lay in the path of the most obvious drainage route: from the east side of the convent south to Mission Street. Test trenches were strategically located to verify the previous work and to assess the effect of the proposed drain on any discovered structures.

The solution. Two excavation units were dug in the areas most likely to be damaged by the proposed drain. Although upper portions of two buried foundation walls were located as expected, they were too deep to be significantly damaged, and Fox deemed it "prudent to install the drain."

Archeology at Mission San José

Mission San José y San Miguel de Aguayo is the full name of this mission, justly considered the most beautiful of the San Antonio missions, and home of the famed Rose Window. Through time and neglect the buildings, sculptures, and grounds fell into disarray. By 1928 most of the compound walls and incorporated structures had been flattened, the north wall of the church had collapsed, the stairs to the bell tower had fallen, and the bell tower itself had collapsed. What the visitor sees today, with the exception of most of the church and con-vent, the ends and west wall of the granary, and some of the mill and vat, are replicas constructed by the WPA during the thirties (Fig. 23). All that work was done without attention to archeological evidence and there-by represents an excellent example of the fanciful ex-planations that result when historical myth is not tempered with archeological data. This is not to say that the reconstructions are bad. They are not. In fact, they were done with great concern for detail—documentary and architectural detail—but without the important de-tail archeological data could have provided.

The effect that archeologically derived data can have on interpretation is seen in the changing explanations of the purpose of the vat immediately east of the mill. The feature had been considered a leather-tanning vat, until archeological investigations in 1974 brought that interpretation into question.

Leather tanning at the mission was known from histor-ical sources, but those sources did not indicate where or how the tanning took place. Archeological excavations repeatedly demonstrated that although the Indians liv-ing at the mission adopted many Spanish customs, they tended to modify them dramatically to fit their native cul-ture, insofar as elements of both cultures could be blend-ed. Excavations of Indian quarters at a number of missions (the Alamo, for example) have revealed that the Indians continued to hunt deer and other wild species to supplement food supplied by domestic species. Com-parison of prehistoric butchering techniques with historic techniques revealed that Indians often continued to use their old ways to cut and carry carcasses even though they had other methods available. Thus they combined their new diet with traditional foods obtained in a tradi-tional way. Other, more obvious instances of cultural blending (anthropologists call it syncretism) are found in such technologies as pottery and tool manufacture. In pottery making, for example, the Indians maintained their basic techniques while adapting them to Spanish styles. Before the Spanish arrived, the Indians had no

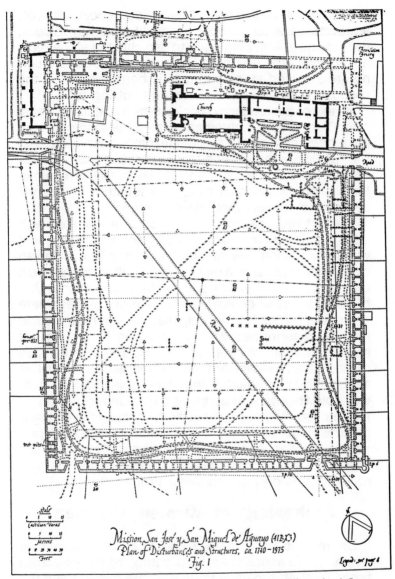

Mission San José y San Miguel de Aguayo (41BX3)
Plan of Disturbances and Structures, ca. 1740–1975
Fig. 1

23. Mission San José. (Map courtesy Texas Historical Commission.)

metal tools and relied on flint for projectile points, knives, and scrapers. After the Spanish established the missions, the Indians at first continued to use chipped stone technology but gradually modified their methods to incorporate iron and steel (particularly barrel hoops) in the production of projectile points and cutting tools.

In view of the tendency for syncretism of cultural traits, J. W. Clark (1976) suggested that leather tanning would have been carried out the old-fashioned way, and that the vat was perhaps not a tanning vat but was, instead, a stone-lined box or vat associated with sugar manufacture, a purely Spanish trait. The location of the vat seemed to support that interpretation.

The vat was constructed in a place associated with other technologies, such as mechanical grinding and water channeling, that had no precursors in local Indian culture and appear in a relatively unadulterated Spanish tradition. Furthermore, we know from documents that there was a *casa de calderas* (house of kettles) where syrup was boiled. It is unlikely that this operation would have been performed within the mission compound, but it likely would have been near a mill, which could have served as a mechanism for juice extraction as well as a grist mill. Following that line of reasoning, Clark (1976) was able to establish a strong case supporting the interpretation of this feature as the remains of the first sugar industry in the state. He concludes that the vat represents part of an *ingenio de azúcar,* a sugar mill, in which sugarcane (a crop at the mission) was squeezed, the juice reduced, and crystallized sugar produced.

Archeology of Mission San Juan

Limited excavation at Mission San Juan has turned up a remarkable series of artifacts dating from pre-Spanish times through the earliest days at the mission and the brief periods of dominion by Mexico and by the Republic of Texas to present times. Examples of the artifacts are on display at a small interpretive center.

Further Reading

Clark, J. W., Jr. 1976. The sugar industry at Mission San José y San Miguel de Aguayo. *Bulletin of the Texas Archeological Society* 51:245–259. Clark gives a beautiful example of how to combine good architecture, archeology, history, ethnography, intuition, and logic into a neat package. It's obvious he had fun doing this. Highly recommended reading.

Fox, A. A. 1988. Archeological investigations at Mission Concepción, Fall of 1986. Archeological Survey Report No. 172. Center for Archeological Research, the University of Texas at San Antonio. This is a good example of modern applied archeology in which a specific problem is outlined, a plan of research is developed and followed, and a recommendation is made.

Fox. D. E. 1983. *Traces of Texas History: Archeological Evidence of the Past 450 Years.* San Antonio: Corona. This is the most comprehensive book dealing with historical archeology in Texas. Chapter 5: Remains of the Spanish Colonial Empire, and Chapter 6: Sites of Mexican Texas, the Revolution, and the Republic, are especially important to those who want a more comprehensive review of archeology in San Antonio. Very good list of recommended readings and references.

Habig, M. A. 1968. *The Alamo Chain of Missions: A History of San Antonio's Five Old Missions.* Chicago: Franciscan Herald Press. This is a must for all Texas history buffs. It is especially important for those interested in the history of San Antonio, Catholicism in Texas, or the Spanish colonial period.

Labadie, J. H. (assembler). 1986. La Villita earthworks (41 BX 677): San Antonio, Texas. Archeological Survey Report No. 158. Center for Archeological Research, the University of Texas at San Antonio. A comprehensive account of the situation leading to the discovery, excavation, and interpretation of a Mexican gun battery, this contains a succinct summary of archival research dealing with Spanish missions and fortifications as well as analyses of military artifacts and ceramics.

Peña, J. E. de la. 1975. *With Santa Anna in Texas: A Personal Narrative of the Revolution.* Translated by Carmen Perry. College Station: Texas A&M University Press. This book is highly recommended to anyone with an interest in the history of Texas-Mexico relations. Peña looks at the Texas revolutionary break with Mexico from a Mexican insider's point of view. Excellent translation. Highly recommended.

Weddle, R. S. 1968. *San Juan Bautista: Gateway to Spanish Texas.* Austin: University of Texas Press. This classic of modern Texas historical literature is highly recommended for anyone interested in the historical archeology of the Spanish colonial period in Texas.

Seminole Canyon State Historical Park
P.O. Box 806
Comstock, Texas 78837
(915) 292-4464

General description: This park is on U.S. Highway 90, about 180 miles west of San Antonio, halfway between Del Rio and Langtry. It consists of more than 2,000 acres of brushland and canyon (Fig. 24). History and archeology are emphasized in a small but excellent interpretive center. One of the most impressive rockshelter sites in Texas is featured here. Guided tours to the Fate Bell Shelter depart from the visitor center at 10 A.M. and 3 P.M. Wednesday through Sunday; the park is closed Mondays and Tuesdays. At the turnaround of a 3 1/2-mile hiking trail, another important site, Panther Cave, may be viewed from the rim overlooking the impressive Rio Grande Canyon.

  Altitude: 1,100 feet above mean sea level
  Average annual precipitation: 17 inches
  Average January minimum temperature: 40°F
  Average July maximum temperature: 94°F

Standard archeological interpretation:
  Site: Fate Bell Shelter (41VV74; site numbers are explained in the section on Hueco Tanks); various
  Type of site: Rockshelter, special-purpose, occupation
  Developmental stage: Hunting and gathering
  Archeological period: Archaic
  Dates: 6000 B.C.–Historic
  Archeological culture: Pecos River Focus
  Diagnostic traits: Pictographs, burned rock middens, sotol and lechuguilla quids, *Pandale, Langtry,* and *Ensor* projectile points

Comment: This part of Texas tends to make one feel like a pioneer. The wide-open spaces, unexpectedly deep canyons, abundant wildlife, and the independent spirit of the people help create an illusion of the Old West. Anyone not familiar with Texas' wide-open spaces may experience some agoraphobia in this part of the state. There aren't many people, and there's a whole lot of land. Generally, the landscape is dominated by gently rolling hills and relatively flat, open brush country dissected by occasional deep canyons.

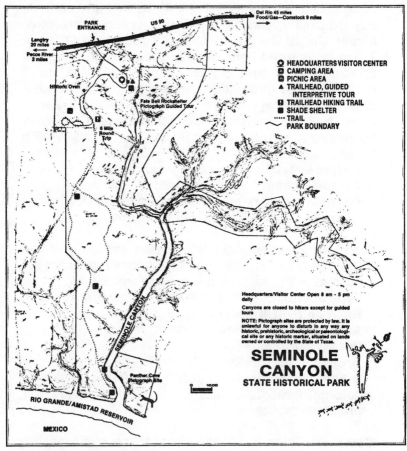

24. Seminole Canyon. (Map courtesy Texas Parks and Wildlife.)

Environment: The park is at the northeastern boundary of the Chihuahuan Desert Province, one of the great modern North American deserts. To the north the desert blends into a shortgrass prairie and semidesert province; a juniper-oak-mesquite savannah province is characteristic of the Hill Country to the east; and a mesquite-acacia savannah prevails to the south. As a consequence of its location, the park area today maintains not only species of plants and animals characteristic of the desert but also many that are typical of the neighboring provinces. The blend of environmental characteristics is one of the most significant features of the park area and the prehistoric cultures that flourished in this part of Texas. Keep in mind that as the climate fluctuated through time, the environment of the area correspondingly changed and boundaries of the various provinces shifted.

Another interesting environmental feature is the scarcity of water. The only reliable year-round sources of water would have been the Pecos River and the Rio Grande. Both supply water from an exotic source; that is, water available from the rivers is derived from a foreign source, in this case the mountains of what is today New Mexico and southern Colorado. Not only was water regularly available in an otherwise desert environment but also the ecology of the canyons and valleys of the streams is strikingly different from that of the surrounding region. There is ample evidence that in the past those features played an important role in human behavior, just as they do today.

Plants: Typical plants include ocotillo, purple sage, sotol, and agave. Ocotillo (*Fouquieria splendens*) is a good example of a xerophytic (drought-resistant) plant. Its long, scraggly branches look dead for most of the year but suddenly come alive with bright green leaves and gaudy red flowers after each infrequent rainstorm. In spite of its normally withered appearance, this is indeed a most useful plant: the Indians used the roots as a poultice for minor burns, cuts, and abrasions; the stems have sometimes been used as fuel (or even walking sticks); the bark contains resin and wax used in the curing of leather; and the flowers and seed pods provide nourishing food.

Purple sage (*Leucophyllum frutescens*) is also known as senisa, cenizo, or barometer bush. It too is an excellent example of a plant well adapted to a dry habitat. Its normally ashy-gray leaves turn greener, and its violet to purple flowers typically spring into bloom when the atmospheric pressure drops preceding a rainstorm (hence the term "barometer bush"). In this way the plant has time to complete its reproductive cycle between rains. A tea brewed from the leaves is used for chills and fever.

Several species of agave are quite common. These plants are similar to those used in modern Mexico for the production of tequila, mescal, and pulque. One, *Agave lecheguilla,* is most frequent and appears throughout the park as a cluster of short, thick, inward-curving leaves, often with a tall spinelike stalk. The scientific name derives from the Greek word *agaue,* meaning "noble," and the Spanish word *lechuguilla,* meaning "little lettuce." The plant has been used in both historic and prehistoric times as a source of food and fiber. Many of the fibrous quids at the Fate Bell Shelter are the remains of lechuguilla feasts in which the base of the plant was cooked and eaten in much the same fashion as we eat artichokes today. Fittingly enough, the local name for *Agave lecheguilla* is "Indian artichoke."

Sotol (*Dasylirion* spp.) is also quite common in the park. It is distinguished by long, slender, serrated green leaves clumped around a short, woody trunk. White or light green flowers appear at the end of a 4-to-6-foot spike growing from the center of the clump of leaves. This plant was also eaten in much the same fashion as artichokes. Many of the burned rocks at the Fate Bell and other sites in the area are from sotol pits, where sotol and lechuguilla were cooked. Fiber from the plants was used in the manufacture of sandals, twine, baskets, and mats.

Other useful plant parts that have been found at Fate Bell and other sites in the area include prickly pear tunas (the dark red fruit of the prickly pear cactus), mesquite seeds, piñon nuts, acorns, sunflower seeds, yucca, and hackberry. In addition to plants used for food and fiber, mescal beans (from *Sophora secundiflora*) and peyote (*Lophophora williamsii*) were ritually used for their hallucinogenic properties (see the discussion of pictographs at the end of this chapter).

Animals. White-tailed deer, javelina, scaled and Gambel's quail, jackrabbit, kangaroo rat, coyote, bobcat, redtailed hawk, diamondback rattlesnake, centipede, tarantula, and scorpion are all characteristic of the region today. It is not unusual to discover two or three centipedes and a kangaroo rat or two trapped in an excavation pit when returning to a dig in the early morning. A large rockshelter site not far from the Fate Bell Shelter is called Coon Tail Spin after the local term for diamondback rattlesnakes, known as "coontails" because the characteristic black and gray bands just before the rattle resemble a raccoon tail. Don't worry, you probably won't encounter any of them in the park unless you deliberately look for one.

Archeology: This park contains some of the clearest examples of important features of the archeology of this region. Work in the area during the last 25 years, mostly in conjunction with construction of Lake Amistad, has created an intriguing but vastly incomplete glimpse of lifeways over a period of about 10,000 years. An outline of the understanding of much of this work is well represented in the interpretive center and is included in Chapter 4 of this book. It is safe to say that the bulk of the evidence of prehistoric occupation derives from the Archaic period.

An intensive survey of the 2,100 acres of the park in 1980 discovered and reported 38 previously unrecorded sites. Approximately 70 sites have now been identified within the park, but it is likely that even more sites will be identified in the future and that others will be lost, because of several characteristics of archeology mentioned previously: artifactual material becomes observable (or lost) through the effects of erosion, archeologists learn what to look for and therefore can find material previously unrecognized, they have time to look more thoroughly, and the definition of "site" sometimes changes. All those characteristics figure in the current count of archeological sites within Seminole Canyon.

Of the sites currently recognized, there are 18 designated as rock art sites, 8 rockshelters, 5 quarries, 14 burned rock middens, 4 scatters, 12 alignments, and 8 historic sites. Most are not currently open to public visitation. Although park plans include ongoing display excavations and new areas open to the public, lack of money has delayed the developments. This discussion will focus on rock art and rockshelters, since both are currently open to the general public for viewing.

Rockshelters. The term "rockshelter" refers to an area sheltered from the elements by a rock overhang. There are a large number of such sites in Texas, but nowhere are they more spectacular than in this region. The most spectacular of all is the Fate Bell Shelter (41VV74). It is famous both as a rock art site and as one of the largest rockshelters with extensive deposits of prehistoric materials.

The approach to the site from the canyon floor is truly impressive. The shelter is more than 400 feet long and as much as 120 feet from the dripline (maximum rock overhang from which water would drip straight down) to the back wall, and it dominates the canyon wall below the interpretive center. In front, extending from the floor well down into the canyon, the shelter is marked by a gray talus (rocky slope) of burned limestone and midden soil indicative of the extensive human use of the site.

Although the importance of this magnificent site cannot be fairly represented in a brief guide, the reader is directed to the references at the end of this chapter for further information. Only two important features of the Fate Bell Shelter are of interest here. It is an excellent example of a dry shelter and a spectacular rock art (pictograph) site.

Dry shelter. The term "dry shelter" refers to the protection from the elements provided by the rock overhang, leaving the contents of the site virtually dry for centuries or, perhaps, eons. Such sites usually contain material in a much better state of preservation than is usual in archeological sites. Dry shelters are fairly common in the Rio Grande–Pecos area because of the unusual geography of the region but are rather rare in much of the rest of the state.

As you stroll along the path at the edge of the shelter, note the perishable material throughout the site. It is the type of artifactual material not usually found in open sites and is one of the reasons shelters such as Fate Bell are so interesting and important. Artifacts made from plants include the quids, which are most obvious, basketry, sandals, mats, cords, nets, *atl-atls* (spearthrowers), rabbit sticks, bows, arrow shafts, fire hearths, and drills. Fate Bell, Coon Tail Spin, and other rockshelters in the immediate area have yielded a more extensive inventory of perishable artifacts associated with the Archaic than is characteristic elsewhere in North America.

Pictographs. The paintings associated with the Archaic in this area are well represented within the Seminole Canyon park. Taken as a whole, the paintings (pictographs) are perhaps the earliest, most comprehensive body of prehistoric art in the New World. Although the meanings of these great combinations of line, color, and design are lost in antiquity, perhaps never again to be realized in the original sense, it is tempting to guess what the artists had in mind when they created these paintings several thousand years ago. W. W. Newcomb's classic analysis of the Pecos River art styles (Newcomb 1967) and the more recent and comprehensive study of the Seminole Canyon area by H. J. Shafer and others (1986) are highly recommended for those who wish to pursue the interpretations of the paintings in greater depth. In general it seems the paintings represent themes common to hunting and gathering societies. The artists seemed to be concerned with insuring the success of the hunt by invoking magical powers. They were interested in exerting some sort of magical power over deer and other animals and are thought to have been part of a psychedelic peyote or mescal bean cult. The figures are often depicted as holding a spearthrower (*atl-atl*) and pouchlike objects resembling prickly pear pads. Four periods of Pecos River art have been identified.

Period 1 (Middle Archaic). These earliest paintings are crude, simple, red humanlike figures that are now badly faded and not well represented in the park.

Period 2 (Middle-Late Archaic). The characteristic Pecos style is manifest in this period. The figures representing shamans are mere outlines of figures with little or no head, vertical legs, and arms held horizontally. The outline figures tend to be among the largest of any of the four periods. Large, naturalistic figures of cougars and deer are also characteristic of this period.

Period 3 (Late Archaic). Shamans in this period are most often painted in two colors, usually red and black, with the outline form often half-filled with color. The figures are almost all less than 6 feet high and usually have heads clearly represented. This style is well represented in the Fate Bell Shelter.

Period 4 (Late Archaic). Shaman representations of this period are highly stylized figures that are often accompanied by dots or circles.

In addition to the shaman figures, various animals such as deer, puma, porcupines, and catfish are represented in all periods. Other designs suggest boats, combs, bows, arrows, and, perhaps, plants. All in all, these representations seem to be associated with a hunting and gathering economy.

Although it is not surprising that Archaic peoples would be concerned with symbolic representations of things in the natural environment that they contended with daily, it is certainly unusual that they had the resources to develop and maintain such a sophisticated art style over such a long time.

Perhaps we will never know what these paintings meant to those who painted them. Considering the debate over the meaning of modern paintings, that is not too surprising. It may be argued that the major function of the paintings today is to provide a projection screen against which we may study our own cultural imperatives.

Further Reading

Of the various references that deal with the archeology of Texas, I have found the following to be most helpful in providing information about this area.

Newcomb, W. W. 1967. *Rock art of Texas Indians.* Austin: University of Texas Press. This excellent book is the most complete presentation of prehistoric rock art in Texas. Featuring the field drawings and paintings of the late Forrest Kirkland of Dallas, it is a collector's item. Highly recommended.

Shafer, H. J. 1986. *Ancient Texans: Rock Art Along the Lower Pecos.* Austin: Texas Monthly Press. This volume is wonderfully illustrated and contains some of the most up-to-date interpretations and descriptions of the culture of the Lower Pecos peoples. Highly recommended.

Turner, Ellen Sue, and Thomas R. Hester. 1985. *A Field Guide to Stone Artifacts of Texas Indians.* Austin: Texas Monthly Press. A useful guide to dates, cultures, and artifacts of Texas prehistory throughout the state. Highly recommended.

SOUTH TEXAS REGION

The South Texas plains, noted in song and literature as the home of the vaquero, the cowboy, impart a distinctive flavor to human existence there. Archeological evidence indicates that this cultural quality was characteristic of the earliest human occupants of the area. Their hunting and gathering adaptation was so efficient that it was maintained long after European contact. South Texas sites offer excellent opportunities to study hunting and gathering societies before they were influenced by food producers.

The southern limit of this great delta-shaped region is defined by the Gulf of Mexico and the Rio Grande; the

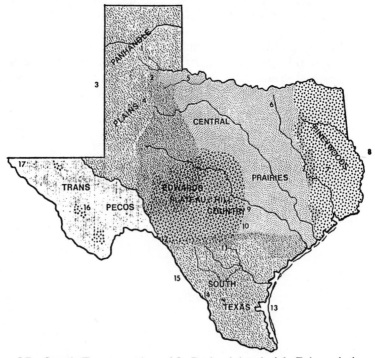

25. South Texas region. 13. Padre Island. 14. Falcon Lake. 15. San Juan Bautista.

northern limits blend into the Pineywoods in the northeast and into the Central Prairies in the north and northwest (Fig. 25). Although there are thousands of sites in the region, only three locations are described here. They are the Padre Island shipwrecks site, Falcon Lake, and the village of Vicente Guerrero.

Padre Island National Seashore
9405 S. Padre Island Drive
Corpus Christi, Texas 78418
(512) 949-8173

General description: In Corpus Christi go east on S. Padre Island Drive, cross Laguna Madre on the JFK Causeway, and turn right on Park Road 22. It is about 9 miles to the Malaquite Beach visitor center. Even though the general location of the Padre Island Spanish shipwrecks has been known for a long time, the exact location was lost from public knowledge until the late sixties, when a treasure-hunting firm began salvage operations. Sensational accounts of Spanish treasure ships so aroused public interest that the State Antiquities Code was passed in 1969 to protect these and other important archeological sites in Texas. The beach adjacent to the shipwreck areas is part of the Padre Island National Seashore.

The park, almost 68 miles of beaches, dunes, and grasslands over more than 130,000 acres, is currently managed by the National Park Service (Fig. 26). Visitors will find a ranger station and basic facilities at the relatively accessible northern end of the park. Most of the rest of the park requires a determined effort to visit and can be quite hazardous for the unprepared. Be sure to check in with the park rangers before exploring areas of the park not easily reached from the paved road.

Altitude: Sea level to 40 feet above mean sea level
Average annual precipitation: 26 inches
Average January minimum temperature: 50°F
Average July maximum temperature: 96°F
Standard archeological interpretation:
  Site: Sixteenth-century Spanish shipwrecks
  Type of site: Incidental
  Developmental stage: Historic
  Archeological period: Historic
  Date: April 1554
  Archeological culture: Spanish
  Diagnostic traits: Ship's gear, cargo, personal items

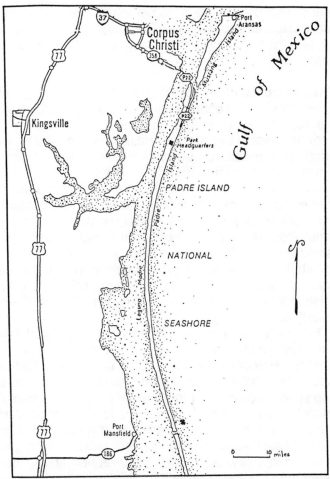

26. Padre Island National Seashore. *X* marks the approximate location of sixteenth-century Spanish shipwrecks.

Comment: There are many places on Padre Island where historic and prehistoric materials can be found, but the sixteenth-century Spanish shipwrecks are certainly the most famous. Although the shipwrecks themselves are offshore at the southern end of the park near the Mansfield Cut, almost any place along the beach will give the feel of those sites. As a barrier island, Padre Island affords unusual opportunities for study in ecology, geology, history, and the glamorous, high-tech field of nautical archeology.

Environment: The Texas coast affords many opportunities to study present and immediately past environments, and Padre Island National Seashore is truly a national treasure in that regard. Active biologic and geologic processes can be observed in a natural setting where human intervention is minimal.

Padre Island is the largest of a series of barrier islands that make the Texas Gulf coast so scientifically interesting. Barrier islands typically form coasts that are separated from the mainland by a sheltered lagoon. Padre Island is one of the largest such islands in the world, and the sheltered lagoon, Laguna Madre, is among the largest such lagoons. Barrier-lagoon coasts of this type comprise about 10 per cent of the world's continental coastline.

There is widespread agreement that the present Texas coastline was formed mainly during the Pleistocene (Ice Age) and Holocene (modern) times, but there is also considerable debate concerning the geophysical processes and specific time periods. Generally, the processes are associated with fluctuations in sea level correlated with the alternating growth and retreat of glacial ice during the Ice Age. Climatic variation in temperature, wind direction and velocity, ocean current direction and velocity, sediment size and composition, and variation in sea level are among the factors that have been considered in the development of a series of coastlines, of which Padre Island is part of the most recent. Earlier, but now submerged, barrier islands similar to Padre Island extend more than 100 miles into the present Gulf of Mexico. Perhaps someday archeology will prove useful in dating the sequence of development of those barriers.

There are a large number of types of environments along the Texas Gulf coast, each with its own community of plants and animals. Three habitats characteristic of the barrier islands are the protected landward, lagoon side of the island; the interior; and the open ocean, beach area.

Archeology: Without doubt, the archeological significance of Padre Island consists of the various shipwrecks that have occurred in that area of the Gulf of Mexico in the fairly recent past. The best-known wreck occurred in 1554 when three Spanish ships sailing from San Juan de Ulua, the port of modern Vera Cruz, Mexico, were driven ashore by a springtime storm. The wrecks provide good examples of incidental sites, historic archeology, and nautical archeology.

Incidental sites. If incidental sites are seen as those places where artifacts were deposited as a consequence of unintended forces, then the shipwrecks off Padre Island must surely be classic examples. Such sites permit the study of human behavior in ways the actor had not intended. The shipwrecks offer microcosms of life in the Spanish New World and upon Spanish vessels in the sixteenth century, not only in terms of the listed, intended cargo but also in terms of other, perhaps originally concealed cargo, which was left aboard the sinking vessel in the haste to abandon ship. For example, personal possessions recovered from the wrecks include religious objects that were not on the cargo manifest and probably would not have been known had they not been tragically abandoned. Their study provides insight into technology as well as religion of the times. Many of them, such as gold crosses and chalices, might reasonably have been predicted on a ship operated by devout Catholics.

Some of the objects are much more mysterious, however, and cannot be explained so simply. Among the more interesting of the recovered religious artifacts are an iron pyrite mirror, four obsidian blades, and an obsidian bead. Iron pyrite is popularly referred to as fool's gold. The mirror fashioned from iron pyrite is several inches in diameter and has beveled edges and a highly polished surface. Mirrors of this type were common in ceremonial centers in Mexico from Olmec times (800 B.C.). In the

Valley of Mexico they were associated with the great god Tezcatlipoca, the god of the smoking mirror. Obsidian, a volcanic glass, was widely traded in prehistoric Mexico in the form of long, narrow, carefully prepared flakes known to archeologists as "blades." Obsidian blades were often modified into knives or projectile points, or since such blades typically have extremely sharp edges, they were used as cutting tools without further modification. Obsidian is still widely used in the manufacture of beads in Mexico.

The items were associated with religion in the Valley of Mexico and elsewhere in Mesoamerica. Could they represent some of the booty stolen from an ancient Aztec tomb in much the same way that King Tutankhamen's tomb was vandalized before Howard Carter excavated it? Were the shipwrecks the result of a curse attached to the items from the desecrated tomb? Are they related to the gloomy prophecy of a priest who sailed on one of the doomed ships? Probably not. Their presence may signify nothing more than an early example of the well-known modern habit of souvenir collecting. In any event, items such as these may provide insights into the habits of past cultures, and that is why they, and the context they are found in, have more value as part of the archeological record than they can ever have apart from that record.

Historical archeology. The combination of history and archeology offers exciting opportunities to cross-check from one discipline to the other. In the case of the Spanish shipwrecks at Padre Island, the abundance of historical detail about the ships, their crews, cargoes, points of origin, destination, and so on gives archeologists an idea of what to look for and how to interpret what they find.

Historical documents indicate that four ships—the *Espiritu Santo,* commanded by Damien Martin, the *San Estaban,* commanded by Francisco del Huerto, the *Santa Maria de Yciar,* commanded by the owner, Miguel de Jauregui, and the *San Andres,* commanded by Captain-General Antonio Corzo—set sail from San Juan de Ulua on April 9, 1554. The *San Andres* was the only one to reach port at Havana. Subsequent documents indicate that about 300 of the 410 people who boarded the ships perished when the three missing ships were driven ashore by gales.

The *Santa Maria's* records indicate she carried 40 passengers and a crew of 27. Of the passengers 34 were men and 6 were women. Five of the men and one woman were slaves, two men and one woman were prisoners, and one man was a priest. In view of what happened to the little armada, it is interesting to note that one of the priests sailing on one of the other ships issued this prophecy: "Woe to those of us who are going to Spain, because neither we nor the fleet will arrive there. Most of us will perish, and those who are left will experience great torment, though all will die in the end except very few" (Davis 1977:18).

Thus, on the one hand, historical documents can provide a basis of expectation for archeological search and interpretation. On the other hand, archeology can provide information not usually recorded and thereby provide a basis for reevaluation, if not revision, of historical data. For example, a species of New World cockroach was found in the conglomerate of material from one of the ships. Since roaches were not on the manifest, and since the species had not been known in Europe before the Spanish colonization of Mexico, we might infer that representatives of this species of roach were stowaways that countercolonized Europe—a trivial example, perhaps, but graphically illustrative of the potential of the interplay between history and archeology.

Nautical archeology. Nautical archeology is a branch of archeology centered around human use of the sea. It includes the study of ships, shipping, cargoes, marine technology, docks, navigation, and all other aspects of the relationship between the sea and human culture. Its most obvious difference from dryland archeology is that much of nautical archeology is done in the sea. Excavation of an underwater shipwreck is vastly different from excavation of a dryland site. The Padre Island Spanish shipwrecks provide particularly good sites because they are rather spectacular, are near at hand, and can be historically identified. Before their rediscovery in the late sixties, there was almost no nautical archeology in Texas. Since then several Texas institutions have developed various aspects of nautical archeology, the most eminent being the world-class program in nautical archeology at Texas A&M University.

Further Reading

Arnold, J. Barto III, and R. Weddle. 1978. *The Nautical Archeology of Padre Island: The Spanish Shipwrecks of 1554.* New York: Academic Press. Going beyond the treasure-ship approach, this book is a somewhat detailed description of some of the early work done in marine archeology in Texas. It contains a good historic account of shipwrecks by Weddle.

Davis, J. L. 1977. *Treasure, People, Ships and Dreams: A Spanish Shipwreck on the Texas Coast.* Austin: Texas Antiquities Committee, and San Antonio: Institute of Texan Cultures. A readable, popular account of the wrecks—their history, archeology, and conservation. Well illustrated. Recommended.

Olds, D. L. 1976. Texas Legacy From the Gulf: A Report on Sixteenth-Century Shipwreck Materials Recovered From the Texas Tidelands. Miscellaneous Papers No. 5, Texas Memorial Museum; Publication No. 2, Texas Antiquities Committee, Austin. A comprehensive account of the artifacts recovered from the shipwreck believed to be that of the *Santa Maria de Yciar,* with illustrations, descriptions, catalogs.

Falcon State Recreation Area
P.O. Box 48
Falcon Heights, Texas 78545
(512) 848-5327

General description: The park is near the dam at Falcon Lake, in the western corner of Starr County on Park Road 46, just off Farm Road 2098 west of U.S. Highway 83 about 75 miles south of Laredo. Falcon Lake (87,000 acres) was constructed as a joint project of the federal governments of the United States and Mexico and is managed by the International Boundary and Water Commission. Although the Falcon State Recreation Area consists of only about 570 acres under the control of the Texas Parks and Wildlife Department, most of the entire lake area is readily accessible for exploration.

The park, as the official name indicates, is primarily intended as a recreation area. Therefore, little money has been dedicated for other purposes. Although there are no exhibits, and sites in the park area have been severely disturbed, some to the point of total destruction of evidence, the Falcon area has considerable archeological significance (Fig. 27). There are screened shelters, bathrooms and showers, and facilities for camping, boat launching, fish cleaning, and picnicking, but there are no interpretive exhibits, nature walks, or other informative assistance unrelated to recreation. If you are interested in such pursuits, you must come prepared. For those who are prepared, Falcon is well worth a visit.

    Altitude: 370 feet above mean sea level
    Average annual precipitation: 17 inches
    Average January minimum temperature: 46°F
    Average July maximum temperature: 100°F

Standard archeological interpretation:
    Site: Various
    Type of site: Open camps
    Developmental stage: Hunting and gathering
    Archeological period: Archaic

Dates: 5000 B.C.–Historic contact
Archeological culture: Falcon Focus, Mier Focus
Diagnostic traits: *Tortugas, Abasolo, Catan, Matamoros* dart points

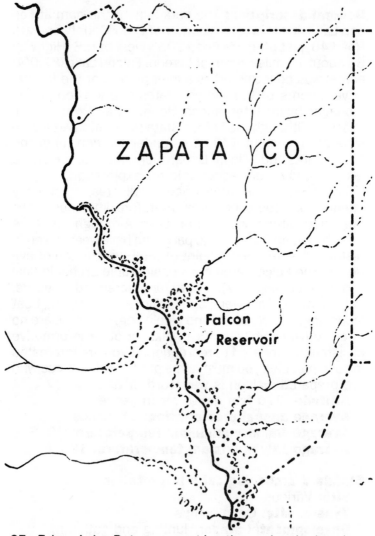

27. Falcon Lake. Dots represent hunting and gathering sites in Falcon area.

Comment: This area, lying as it does in the wide-open spaces between the population centers of the Lower Rio Grande Valley and San Antonio, is among the least-populated regions of Texas. The counties southwest of San Antonio are all heavily influenced by Mexico, and those along the border (such as Starr and Zapata counties, where Falcon Lake is located) are very Mexican. Similarly, areas of Mexico immediately south of the Rio Grande are much like Texas in many ways. This complementary similarity has a long history. People on both sides of the border recognize their close relationship and have at various times suggested withdrawing from their respective nations and forming a new country of their own.

Environment: One of the most important elements in archeological interpretation is the environment, and the relationship between it and cultures is most easily observed in this area of Texas. The Falcon area holds a significant clue to the fragile relationship between human cultural adaptation and ecological change. In the not too distant past, this part of Texas had one of the largest human populations in the state; obviously, the situation has drastically changed so that today the region is among the least populated. A close inspection of the modern environment will determine if the changes have been environmental, cultural, or both.

This part of Texas and northeastern Mexico is clearly within the Gulf Coastal Plain, a vast area of gently undulating hills traversed by the Rio Grande. Occasional sharply delineated rock outcroppings of low relief occur throughout the area but are commonly found along major streams and in the uplands.

Although the Rio Grande maintains a flow of water from distant sources, its tributaries are dependent on local precipitation and are ephemeral. Some of them have water holes with water year-round, but fluctuations in water quality render them unreliable as sources of food or water for long periods. In the past the river seems to have been the only reliable source of water, at least since the periods of greater precipitation associated with the latter stages of the most recent glaciation. Clearly, the Rio Grande today provides the only constant source of water in the region, and in spite of significant environmental changes in historic times, it was similarly crucial in the past. Thus, the river has been the single most significant factor in determining the region's patterns of life, including human cultural patterns.

Three distinct zones, the vega, the lomeria, and the mesa, can be observed in the immediate vicinity of the river and Falcon State Recreation Area. Each zone provided resources for prehistoric inhabitants, and an understanding of them is important to the understanding of the archeology of South Texas.

Vega zone. The first zone lies nearest the river in the form of alluvial terraces. The terraces are relatively flat and are bisected by deep, steep-sided arroyos where tributaries enter the river. Although this zone is covered by the water of Falcon Lake and is not presently visible at Falcon State Recreation Area, the brush-covered vega is clearly visible on both sides of the river downstream from the dam as well as upstream from the lake. Before completion of the dam, this zone was subject to periodic and unexpected flooding.

Besides the present channel of the river, the vega is marked by numerous resacas, relatively permanent ponds formed within abandoned river channels. The frequency of resacas increases with the decrease in gradient as the river approaches the Gulf and are more common along this stretch of the Rio Grande than they are farther upstream near Guerrero (described later in this chapter) or Seminole Canyon (described in the chapter on the Edwards Plateau/Hill Country).

The plant community of the vega is adapted to a greater amount of moisture than the annual rainfall of the region could normally supply. The extra water, of course, comes from the river, which does not depend on local precipitation. Trees commonly found in the vega include retama (*Parkinsonia aculeata*), Texas ebony (*Pithecellobium flexicaule*), black willow (*Salix nigra*), cedar elm (*Ul-*

mus crassifolia), cottonwood (*Populus deltoides*), and huisache (*Acacia farnesiana*).

Besides a great variety of fish, amphibians, mollusks, and other aquatic animal species limited to the permanent waters of the river and resacas, the vega is home to a number of mammals that do not range far from water. They include beaver (*Castor canadensis*), raccoon (*Procyon lotor*), and alligator (*Alligator mississipiensis*).

Lomeria zone. The second major zone is formed by the hilly territory flanking the river and its tributaries. Perhaps because of its convenient location between the resources of the two other zones, it was the favorite zone for human habitation in prehistoric times. The Falcon State Recreation Area is situated in this zone and provides excellent examples of characteristic plants and animals.

Originally, the vegetation on the area was dominated by short and medium grasses and woody shrubs, but that climax vegetation has largely been replaced by woody invaders. The characteristic growth consists of the spiny shrubs and stunted trees of the famed brush country, or chaparral, of South Texas. Dominant woody species include mesquite (*Prosopis glandulosa*), black brush (*Acacia rigidula*), and guajillo (*Acacia berlandieri*). Cacti include hedgehog cactus (*Echinocereus pentalophus*), devil's pincushion (*Homalocephala texensis*), and peyote (*Lophophora williamsii*).

Animals found in the lomeria include jackrabbit (*Lepus californicus*), opossum (*Didelphis mesamericana*), western spotted skunk (*Spilogale gracilis*), striped skunk (*Mephitis mephitis*), nine-banded armadillo (*Dasypus novemcinctus mexicanus*), and coatimundi (*Nasua narica*).

Mesa zone. This zone consists of the flat uplands that seem to stretch to the horizon in all directions. Water is scarce here most of the year, but it is especially precious during the dry season. Except for numerous quarries and chipping stations, relatively few archeological sites have been found in the mesa. They are commonly associated with a conspicuous geological feature, the Reynosa formation, which outcrops in the upper elevations throughout the area. It consists of a mixture of rounded and polished pebbles and cobbles in a matrix of sand, sandstone, and clay. The cobbles and pebbles are mostly chert, but they include limestone as well as igneous rocks. There is no question that chert and other stone from the Reynosa formation were the primary raw materials for lithic technology in prehistoric times. Remnants of the Reynosa formation can be found only as caps of the highest hills in the vicinity of Falcon State Recreation Area.

Woody plants characteristic of the upland mesa zone are mesquite (*Prosopis glandulosa*), paloverde (*Cercidium texanum*), guajillo (*Acacia berlandieri*), and cenizo (*Leucophyllum frutescens*). Six-weeks grama (*Bouteloua barbata*) and purple three-awn (*Aristida purpurea*) are dominant modern grasses. Bluebonnet (*Lupinus texensis*) and evening primrose (*Oenothera speciosa*) are common annuals, and blood of the dragon (*Jatropha dioica*) is a hardy perennial.

Characteristic mammals of both the mesa and the Iomeria include javelina (*Tayassu tajacu*), white-tailed deer (*Odocoileus virginianus*), and bobcat (*Lynx rufus*). Other animals include diamondback rattlesnake (*Crotalus atrox*), box turtle (*Terrapene ornata*), banded gecko (*Coleonyx brevis*), and Great Plains skink (*Eumeces obsoletus*).

Archeology: Two important aspects of archeology in Texas are represented quite clearly in the Falcon area. One, salvage archeology, is of interest in terms of the business of archeology. The other, the study of hunting and gathering societies, is of more general concern and holds promise for archeological methodology.

Salvage Archeology

The concept of salvage archeology developed in the late forties as it became obvious that federally funded construction projects were destroying much of the archeological record. Federal monies were at first made available through such agencies as the National Park Service, the River Basin Surveys of the Smithsonian In-

stitution, and the U.S. Bureau of Reclamation. The programs gradually expanded in scope and funding until they
were made an important part of modern environmental
protection legislation. During their tenure, they have been
a major source of funding for archeological work throughout the United States, and so their requirements have
been a determining factor in the development of archeology in Texas. The area that became Falcon Lake was one
of the first reservoir areas in Texas to be surveyed under the auspices of the salvage program. From 1950
through part of 1953, the survey was carried out by what
would later become known as the Texas Archeological
Salvage Project, of the University of Texas at Austin. The
work included a preliminary study of the recent geology
of the lower Rio Grande (Evans 1962). Four terraces were
identified and described: the Reynosa formation, the
Zapata terrace, the Rosita terrace, and the modern floodplain. Of the four, the Zapata and the Rosita are of the
greatest interest archeologically.

Zapata terrace. This is the oldest of the terraces that
contain the few buried sites known in the Falcon area.
It forms a flat surface at an elevation of about 65 feet
above the riverbed, with its base resting on bedrock at
about 30 feet above the riverbed. Cultural material was
discovered in deposits buried as deeply as 18 feet below the surface of this terrace. One of the sites, the Royer
Site, is near the northwest shore of the Falcon State
Recreation Area. Excavations at the Royer Site exposed
a wealth of archeological material, consisting of stone
tools such as knives, preforms, scrapers, and dart point
types (such as *Tortugas* and *Abasolo*) and clearly within
the Archaic period.

Rosita terrace. This terrace occurs as an intermedi-
ate surface between the higher Zapata terrace and the
floodplain and has been interpreted as the middle terrace in a three-terrace series of post–Ice Age deposits
in the area. Many prehistoric sites have been reported
both upon the surface of this terrace as well as buried
in it. At one site near the Falcon park, deposits buried
11 feet below the surface of the Rosita terrace were ra-

diocarbon dated to about 2,700 years ago. *Catan* and *Matamoros* projectile point types are typically reported from these sites.

The Study of Hunting and Gathering Societies
One of the most promising fields in Texas archeology is the study of hunting and gathering societies. As described in Chapter 3, hunting and gathering societies depend on wild species for subsistence; that is, they do not depend on domesticated species for food. Historic and ethnographic sources are useful in establishing a data base concerning such societies but are severely limited in their approach because modern societies, even modern hunting and gathering societies, have been affected to some degree by contact with food-producing societies. Archeology is essential in the study of hunting and gathering societies because it is the only source of information about such societies before they were affected by contact with food producers. Texas, South Texas in particular, has an especially useful supply of such archeological evidence. Based on our current knowledge of the area's archeology, human populations subsisted on hunting and gathering until very recently—the time of historic contact. An abundance of data are readily available in the Falcon Lake area.

Further Reading

Cason, J. F. 1952. Report on archeological salvage in Falcon Reservoir, season of 1952. *Bulletin of the Texas Archeological and Paleontological Society* 23:218–259. One of the few easily obtained accounts of early salvage work in Texas, this report contains a brief account of discoveries in Falcon excavations. Most of the data reported here have subsequently been lost.
Evans, G. L. 1962. Notes on terraces of the Rio Grande, Falcon-Zapata area, Texas. *Bulletin of the Texas Archeological Society* (1961)32:33–45. Evans outlines his preliminary study of the terraces of the Falcon area,

with brief descriptions of each. This is a good example of some of the early work done by archeological salvage programs.

San Juan Bautista del Rio Grande
Guerrero, Coahuila
Mexico

General description: The village of Guerrero is in the Mexican state of Coahuila, about 25 miles southeast of the city of Piedras Negras, sister city of Eagle Pass, Texas. It has had electricity for only three decades and has been connected by paved highway to Piedras Negras ("black stones," a reference to the coal mined in the area) for only 20 years. About a decade ago the road from Guerrero to Nuevo Laredo was paved, so now it is easy to visit the village from Laredo as well as from Eagle Pass.

There was some expectation, one might even say hope, that the modernizations would lead to a tremendous increase in tourism with a corresponding improvement in the local economy. There have been plans for various tourist facilities, but as of this writing, none have been successfully developed. After a meeting between the governors of Coahuila and Texas in 1988, an agreement of economic cooperation was announced in which Guerrero was mentioned specifically. The success of the most recent venture to attract visitors to this historic and charming little town remains to be seen. In the meantime, don't wait for the masses; now is the time to visit. Although there are no overnight facilities available in Guerrero, there are also no tourist traps. Small cafés and stores sell food and snacks, and it is satisfying to down a cool Mexican beer at one of the local establishments after a hot, dusty visit to the local attractions.

The facade of the town at first appears less than attractive, but the ambience of the place grows on those visitors willing to accept what they find. Here, more than most places, advance preparation is necessary to make your visit truly pleasurable. The only official archeological site here is the federally operated site of the Mission of San Bernardo. The mission grounds are generally open during daylight hours, but the schedule is erratic to nonexistent. Other points of interest may be visited at the pleasure of the town's inhabitants so—be nice.

Altitude: 560 feet above mean sea level
Average annual precipitation: 18.5 inches
Average January minimum temperature: 40°F
Average July maximum temperature: 100°F

Standard archeological interpretation:
Site: San Juan Bautista del Rio Grande
Type of site: Village, presidio, missions
Developmental stage: Historic
Archeological period: Historic
Dates: January 1, 1700–present
Archeological culture: Spanish colonial, Mexican
Diagnostic traits: Historic structures; ceramic, glass, and metal artifacts

Comment: This village, today known as Guerrero (more properly, Vicente Guerrero), was one of the most important places in the Spanish colonization of Texas. For more than a hundred years it served as the southern anchor for El Camino Real (the Royal Highway), along which conquistadores, missionaries, and ordinary settlers traveled to establish places such as San Antonio, Goliad, and Nacogdoches in Texas and the Presidio of Los Adaes in Louisiana. Los Adaes (described in the Pineywoods chapter) marked the end of El Camino Real and for 50 years served as the provincial capital of Texas. Although many of those settlements are today larger and more famous, it was San Juan Bautista that served the Spanish as the "gateway to Texas" (Weddle 1968). Later the armies of Mexico, under the direction of Antonio López de Santa Anna, marched through the streets of this little town en route to battle the Tejanos at the mission site of San Antonio de Valero, the Alamo.

Both ends of El Camino Real lie just outside the modern boundaries of the state, but they are included here because they are two of the most important sites of the

Spanish colonial period of Texas history and because, in a manner of speaking, they *are* part of Texas.

Environment: Although J. Frank Dobie wrote *A Vaquero of the Brush Country* with his beloved South Texas in mind, only the Rio Grande divides this part of Mexico from Dobie's cherished homeland. Most of his vivid descriptions are as valid for the area around Guerrero as for his hometown, Cotulla, only 80 miles due east of Guerrero. Readers who would like to get a true sense of this part of North America are referred to this classic bit of Texana.

The area around Guerrero is part of the Rio Grande Plain. The flat, brush-covered plains of South Texas and northeastern Coahuila have been formed through the centuries by the cutting and deposition processes of a succession of great rivers, the most recent of which is the Rio Grande. This huge area of gently rolling hills and vast prairies is marked by occasional sharply delineated rock outcroppings of low relief, both along the streams and their tributaries and in the upland regions, where they represent erosional remnants of almost vanished earlier depositions.

The spring-fed creek that flows through the town was once blocked by a natural travertine dam and formed a small lake that the padres had found so attractive. In a fit of spite over water rights, the owner dynamited the dam several decades ago, thereby draining the lake and resulting in the present situation. The site of the dam can still be seen. Travertine is a type of freshwater limestone that is formed as a flow of warm, carbonate-laden water slows and cools. The solution becomes supersaturated and carbonates precipitate out, forming deposits. Over the years, rather large stone formations can accumulate. The famous Horse Tail Falls, near Monterrey, Nuevo León, Mexico, is an excellent example of a travertine formation. At San Juan Bautista the travertine was quarried for stone used in the construction of various buildings in the settlement. The quarrying activities are evident on the downstream side of the dam.

The area is near the northeastern boundary of the distinctive Coahuiltecan Desert, and its plants and animals are characteristic of that biotic province. There are also examples typically found in the adjacent Tamaulipan province.

Plants. Mesquite (*Prosopis glandulosa*) is by far the most dominant plant and in places covers the ground as far as the eye can see. Other trees include huisache (*Acacia farnesiana*), cat's claw mimosa (*Mimosa biunicifera*), and retama (*Parkinsonia aculeata*). Grasses include six-weeks grama (*Bouteloua barbata*) and purple three-awn (*Aristida purpurea*), and prickly pear (*Opuntia lindheimeri*) and hedgehog cactus (*Echinocereus pentalophus*) are conspicuous cacti.

Animals. Archeological evidence from excavations at Guerrero indicates that early settlers ate many of the species still found in the area. They include mammals such as opossum (*Didelphis virginiana*), cottontail (*Sylvilagus* spp.), javelina (*Tayassu tajacu*), and white-tailed deer (*Odocoileus virginianus*).

Archeology: The entire village of Guerrero represents a living museum. Its most conspicuous historical elements are the eighteenth- and nineteenth-century structures, some in ruins and some still in use, which can be seen throughout the town. Some of them antedate almost all known historic structures in Texas, and many, modified through the centuries, have been in continuous use for more than 200 years. The village offers the visitor a remarkable opportunity to see examples of historical archeology.

Spanish settlement here began when zealous padres arrived on January 1, 1700. They were pleased with the abundance of fresh water in this relatively verdant valley slashing across an otherwise dry plain. Since they first saw this valley on New Year's Day, the day of Christ's circumcision, they named it the Valley of the Circumcision. The first of three missions established here, San Juan Bautista was founded on that same New Year's Day by three Franciscan priests, Antonio Olivares, Marcos de Guerena, and Francisco Hidalgo. They were escorted by twenty soldiers under the command of Sergeant-Major Diego Ramon.

Ramon laid out the ground plan for a second mission, San Francisco Solano, which was founded two months later on the first day of March 1700. That mission was subsequently moved to the village of San Antonio de Bexar, where its name was changed to San Antonio de Valero and its church became known as the Alamo. That most famous of Texas icons had its origin, here, in this humble Mexican village. One of the best reasons to visit Guerrero is to see a place that looks much the same today as San Antonio must have looked during the early part of its existence. Strolling the streets of Guerrero is certainly reminiscent of older sections of San Antonio, La Villita perhaps, but the experience is much more authentic.

The third and final mission established here, San Bernardo, was founded by Diego Ramon and Father Alonzo Gonzalez in 1702. The large, unfinished church that still stands at this site is the single most obvious attraction remaining from the Spanish colonial period. Built during the 1760's under the direction of Father Diego Jimenez, it was the second church for the San Bernardo Mission. The earlier church and all other mission structures have fallen, and little surface evidence of them remains today.

Excavations in 1975 and 1976 by archeologists from the University of Texas at San Antonio discovered the buried remains of some of those earlier structures. Based on an analysis of their finds, the archeologists concluded that the open area just across the street north of the church was occupied by rows of houses built for the Indian acolytes whom, ostensibly, the mission was to serve. Northeast of the standing ruins was the location of the original church as well as living quarters for the priests. The remaining walls and arches and the dome of the baptistry were strengthened, repaired, straightened, and stabilized by the Ministry of Public Works in 1975. The archeological fieldwork and restoration were under the authority and supervision of a Mexican governmental agency, the Instituto Nacional de Antropologia y Historia (INAH).

Spanish settlements were established here in part to give ready access to several points along the Rio Grande where bedrock ridges make it possible to cross the river easily. The fords were as useful to the Spanish in their colonization of Texas as they are today to drug smugglers. An archeological survey of both sides of the river indicated that people have been crossing the river at these natural crossing points since several thousand years before the Spanish arrived.

Quick Guide to Guerrero

This guide is keyed to the map of the village (Fig. 28) and should serve as a general guide to the above-mentioned features as well as several others not previously mentioned. Beginning on the road from Piedras Negras (Highway 2), stay on the highway (left fork) at the sign to the town of Guerrero and begin looking to the left for the ruins of San Bernardo.

Turn left at the sign for the ruins of the second church of Mission San Bernardo (1). The most impressive structure in Guerrero, this building was begun in the mid-eighteenth century but never finished. The Indian quarters are north of the dome; the priests' quarters and first mission church are 200 feet east of the Indian quarters.

Proceed across the highway to a low-water crossing, park at the side of the road, and walk upstream to the travertine dam and quarry site (2). A natural dam once backed water into a small lake, one of most attractive features of the valley. Travertine was quarried here for construction of missions and other structures.

Return to the highway, turn right, and turn right again at the entrance to the village. This street leads to the main plaza and church (3). The center of Presidio del Rio Grande (originally established in 1701) was officially laid out in 1703. Some walls of the original still stand. Santa Anna's troops marched through this plaza on their way to the Alamo. San Juan Bautista (Saint John the Baptist)

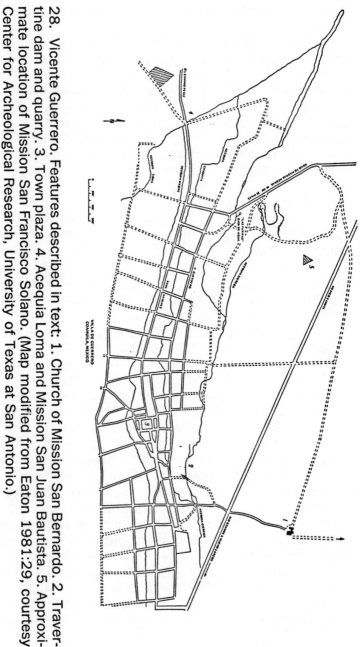

28. Vicente Guerrero. Features described in text: 1. Church of Mission San Bernardo. 2. Travertine dam and quarry. 3. Town plaza. 4. Acequia Loma and Mission San Juan Bautista. 5. Approximate location of Mission San Francisco Solano. (Map modified from Eaton 1981:29, courtesy Center for Archeological Research, University of Texas at San Antonio.)

parish church, on the east side of the plaza, was established early in the eighteenth century. Bells were hung in the bell tower in 1851 in commemoration of the 150th anniversary of the presidio. A small store on the north side of the plaza marks the spot where a soldiers' barracks once stood.

Proceed west from the plaza on Calle Sanchez (this is the original Camino Real) less than half a mile to Acequia Loma and the Mission of San Juan Bautista (4). (Note that the paved road turns north to rejoin Highway 2, but the Camino Real proceeds, unpaved, to the west.) The briskly flowing, embanked stream crossed by a narrow drainage-pipe bridge shortly after the road leaves the pavement is an excellent example of a Spanish colonial irrigation ditch, an acequia. The hill just to the left of the road after it crosses the acequia is the site of the church of the Mission of San Juan Bautista. The exact location of the mission site and structures had been lost until this place was firmly identified by archeological excavations in the mid seventies. *Warning:* Do not leave the road right-of-way at this site. The landowner is out of patience with trespassers, and you could get into serious trouble.

Return to the pavement and turn left. On your way to the highway, you will pass the probable original site of Mission San Francisco Solano (5), the mission that was later moved to San Antonio, where it became San Antonio de Valero, better known as the Alamo.

Further Reading

Castañeda, C. E. 1936. The mission era: The winning of Texas, 1693–1731. *Our Catholic Heritage in Texas,* Vol. 2. Austin: Von Boeckmann-Jones. An immensely valuable source for research into the Spanish colonial period in Texas, this is a collector's item in the original edition. It has also been reprinted. Highly recommended as an important source for further investigation.

Eaton, J. D. 1981. Guerrero, Coahuila, Mexico: A Guide to the Town and Missions. Report No. 4, Center for

Archeological Research, University of Texas at San Antonio. This is a useful bilingual guide to the village of Guerrero. It is written by a key member of the Gateway Project, a general investigation into the archeology and history of the Guerrero area by the Center for Archeological Research. Highly recommended.

Fox, D. E. 1983. *Traces of Texas History: Archeological Evidence of the Past 450 Years.* San Antonio: Corona. This is the most complete volume available on historic archeology in Texas. It is well illustrated and written in clear language. Highly recommended.

Weddle, R. S. 1968. *San Juan Bautista: Gateway to Spanish Texas.* Austin: University of Texas Press. This book remains the definitive statement concerning the history of various aspects of Guerrero. Recommended.

TRANS-PECOS REGION

This is the most mountainous and driest region in Texas. The contrast of basin and range gives it a distinctive appearance and feel. The Trans-Pecos has never sustained a large human population and is today practically unpopulated throughout most of its expanse.

The region is simply defined as all of Texas west of the Pecos River, hence the term "Trans-Pecos." New Mexico forms the northern boundary, and the Rio Grande delineates the border between Texas and its neighboring Mexican states of Coahuila and Chihuahua (Fig. 29).

Although there are a number of important archeological sites in this region, most are not easily accessible, and only two are included in this section: Fort Davis National Historic Site and Hueco Tanks State Historical Park.

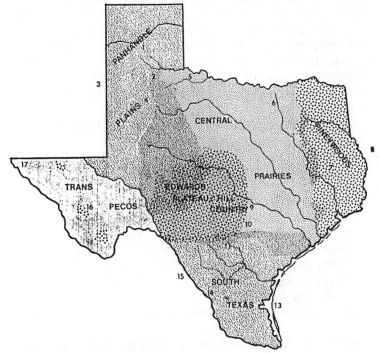

29. Trans-Pecos region. 16. Fort Davis. 17. Hueco Tanks.

Fort Davis National Historic Site
P.O. Box 1456
Fort Davis, Texas 79734
(915) 426-3224

General description: This site is in the northern part of town, just off Texas Highway 17. Its 460 acres were acquired by the National Park Service in 1961. Through the years the park service has excavated, restored, maintained, and interpreted so that today Fort Davis is generally considered one of the best examples of a nineteenth-century frontier fort in the Southwest. A restored barracks has been converted into an excellent visitor center with a museum and a light-and-sound show of the fort's history. Periodically, the parade ground is enlivened by a recorded rendition of an 1875 retreat parade. Costumed park personnel provide information and local color. It is important to begin a visit to the fort at the visitor center to get the latest information about scheduled events. There is a self-guided trail with more than 50 identified stops (Fig. 30). Open 8 A.M.–5 P.M. daily between mid-September and May; 8 A.M.–6 P.M. the rest of the year. Closed Christmas and New Year's Day. Entrance fee is $1 per person, with exceptions.
  Altitude: 4,900 feet above mean sea level
  Average annual precipitation: 19 inches
  Average January minimum temperature: 31°F
  Average July maximum temperature: 82°F

Standard archeological interpretation:
  Site: Fort Davis
  Type of site: Special-purpose, occupational
  Developmental stage: Historic
  Archeological period: Historic
  Dates: 1854–present
  Archeological culture: Historic
  Diagnostic traits: Military structures, hardware

Comment: Jeff Davis County has the highest average elevation of any Texas county, and Fort Davis has the distinction of being the highest town in the state. The weather and scenery in this part of the state are heroic, and the mood is intensified at this grand old infantry and cavalry post. During a stroll across the parade ground, it is not hard to imagine John Wayne barking out the command to "Mount up" as a band of "hostiles" comes riding out of the nearby Limpia Canyon.

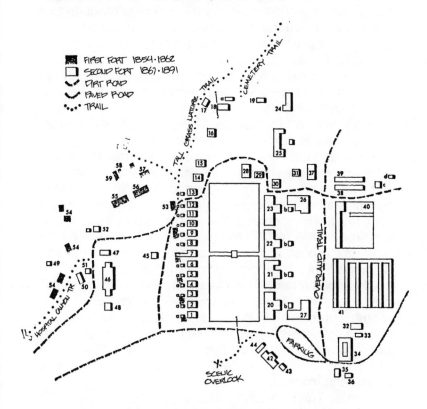

30. Fort Davis. (Map courtesy National Park Service.)

Environment: Fort Davis is characteristic of middle elevations within the basin-and-range type of physiographic province occupied by the Trans-Pecos. Lower elevations are desert basins, and higher elevations tend toward mountainous ranges. Mid-range sites such as Fort Davis often have moderate aspects of both the desert basins and the mountain ranges, resulting in a fragile but delightful environment. Human life here is tenuous and marked by emotional peaks and valleys that seem to be psychological reflections of the environment.

The Davis Mountains represent an isolated, southern extension of the Rocky Mountains. Locally, the topography is characterized by bench formations caused by erosion of softer beds interlayered with harder, erosion-resistant formations. The effect is that of a staircase of benches and escarpments, with abrupt cliffs and canyons and trailing slopes. The sloping surfaces are covered with a coarse scree of weathered volcanic rock and feldspar crystals. Valley soils are derived from volcanic parent material. Andesite, rhyolite porphyry, and ignimbrite are the major types of volcanic rock in the immediate area of the fort. The rugged cliffs of Sleeping Lion Mountain, south of the parade ground, are a dramatic display of the rhyolite porphyry of the area.

Of various igneous rocks used in the construction of the fort, ignimbrite was preferred. For example, the light orange, orange-pink, pink, and light gray walls of the houses on officer's row are made of the material, as are the stone foundations of most of the adobe structures. The adobe itself is full of feldspar crystals and fragments of volcanic rock.

Plants. The park is in a typical juniper-oak savannah characterized by clusters of oak (*Quercus* spp.) and scattered one-seed juniper (*Juniperus monosperma*) with occasional juniper thickets. Smaller woody plants include evergreen sumac (*Rhus virens*), fragrant sumac (*Rhus aromatica*), cholla (*Opuntia imbricata*), and catclaw (*Acacia greggii*). Grasses include Indian ricegrass (*Oryzopsis hymenoides*) and fluffgrass (*Erioneuron pulchellum*).

Animals. The wide variety of birds in the Davis Mountains includes the common cowbird (*Molothrus ater*), Scott's oriole (*Icterus parisorum*), cactus wren (*Campylorhynchus brunneicapillum*), canyon wren (*Catherpes mexicanus*), and lesser goldfinch (*Spinus psaltria*). The area is a veritable birdwatcher's paradise. Other animals include mule deer (*Odocoileus hemionus*), pronghorn antelope (*Antilocapra americana*), coyote (*Canis latrans*), and mountain lion (*Felis concolor*).

Archeology: Historical archeology has been the major concern at Fort Davis. The historical records are relatively complete but lack detail in many areas. Archeology has been used to supply some of that detail. In other areas archeological techniques can supply general information, and history supplies the detail. For example, the records quite clearly indicate that soldiers of the 8th Infantry, under the command of Lt. Colonel Washington Seawell, began construction of the first fort on October 7, 1854, the day they arrived; that the first fort was abandoned by United States troops and occupied by Confederate troops during the civil war (during this interval it was destroyed); that on July 1, 1867, the site was again occupied by U.S. soldiers of the 9th Cavalry and the 24th Infantry, and construction of the second fort began; and that the fort had been constructed to its present appearance by 1875.

Major archeological excavations were carried out in the early stages of park development. Recovered artifacts have been worked into the displays in the museum, and the excavations supported the following conclusions. 1. Two forts were indeed built at Fort Davis. 2. The first fort occupied the area of the general hospital. It contained many temporary structures, had no stockade, and was abandoned in an orderly manner. No archeological evidence was found that related to the reasons for abandonment, but temporary structures of the fort were burned to the ground some time after it was abandoned. 3. The second fort was constructed in the late 1860's.

Thus, the archeological evidence is found to support historical records in most cases. Although the historical records concerning Fort Davis are especially abundant, and many things turned up by the archeologist's shovel seem redundant, the evidence can be significant in determining matters of detail. For example, the positive identification of the soldiers' barracks of the first fort depended, in part, on the superposition of the line of the Officers' Row of the second fort across the foundation line of the barracks from the first fort. An observant visitor can see many instances of superposition in the walls and wall outlines of various structures at the park.

Excavation allows accumulation of many details of everyday existence that might have been considered too trivial (or too embarrassing) for history to record. Excavation of a latrine, for example, usually produces many small artifacts that were accidentally dropped in and were not considered worthwhile to recover (eyeglasses, for example) as well as material that may have been used secretly and disposed of in the privacy of the privy (whiskey bottles, for example). Readers who would like more information about the utility of archeology supplying this sort of detail are referred to W. H. Rathje's garbageology project listed below.

Further Reading

There are no readily available sources that deal with archeology at Fort Davis. The following publications are of some help in the history of the fort.

Day, J. M. 1966. Fort Davis. In *Frontier Forts of Texas,* Colonel H. B. Simpson, coordinator. Waco: Texian Press.

Miller, Ray. 1985. *Ray Miller's Texas Forts: A History and Guide.* Austin: Cordovan Press.

Rathje, W. H. 1974. The Garbage Project: A New Way of Looking at the Problems of Archaeology. *Archaeology* 27:236–241. One of the outstanding examples of the experimental approach to archeological analysis, Rathje's insights were developed from a class exercise. This article is useful in understanding archeology's potential to supply information that can supplement history.

Hueco Tanks State Historical Park
Hueco Tanks Road
Rural Route 3, Box 1
El Paso, Texas 79935
(915) 857-1135

General description: This park is in far West Texas, in El Paso County. To get there from El Paso, take U.S. Highway 62/80 about 26 miles east to the junction with Texas Ranch Road 2775, which leads to the park. The 860 acres include three exposed masses of a form of granite, syenite porphyry, the remains of an intrusion of molten rock into older, sedimentary strata. When the older rocks such as limestones and sandstones were eroded away, the three masses of harder, erosion-resistant syenite remained. Large hollowed areas in the surface of the syenite collect water and are responsible for the major attraction of the park. Fresh water, an important commodity in the desert, is available here. "Hueco" is a Spanish term for "hollow," hence the name "Hueco Tanks."

The park has hiking trails, campsites with utilities, picnic shelters, restrooms with showers, a small interpretive center, and a playground (Fig. 31). Popular activities include picnicking, hiking, rock climbing, nature study, and archeological tours. Admission is $2 per car, and camping is $9 per night for parties of eight or less. The park office is generally open daily from 8 A.M.–5 P.M., but the hours vary according to anticipated activity.

Altitude: 3,750 feet above mean sea level
Average annual precipitation: 7.7 inches
Average January minimum temperature: 32°F
Average July maximum temperature: 94°F

Standard archeological interpretation:
Site: Hueco Tanks (41EP2)
Type of site: Rockshelter; village; special-purpose
Developmental stage: Agriculture
Archeological period: Late Prehistoric
Dates: A.D. 1150–A.D. 1350

Archeological culture: Doña Ana Phase of the Jornada Branch of the Mogollon Culture
Diagnostic traits: Plain and polychrome pottery; adobe houses; round and rectangular pit houses; chipped, ground, and polished stone tools

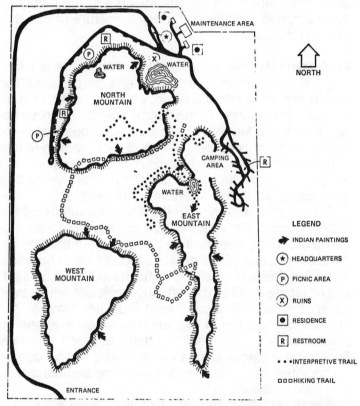

31. Hueco Tanks. (Map courtesy Texas Parks and Wildlife.)

Comment: The volcanic rocks marking this location have attracted visitors for thousands of years. Thrusting more than 400 feet above the basin floor, they are islands of life in the surrounding desert lowlands and offer water, refuge, and hope. In historic times ranchers used this place, the Butterfield Overland Stage stopped here, and various groups have camped here temporarily. Prehistoric peoples may have first come here when Pleistocene megafauna such as mammoth, camels, and giant bison roamed the intermountain basins. Subsequent prehistoric occupations included agriculturalist villagers who probably were responsible for the majority of the paintings that comprise the most remarkable feature of this dramatic state park.

Environment: The park lies within the southeastern fringe of the basin-and-range physiographic province. The park is part of the Hueco Basin, which is itself an extension of a much larger feature known as the Tularosa Basin. The Hueco Mountains are a conspicuous feature of the eastern horizon, and the 7,000-foot Franklin Mountains form the far western horizon. Soils in the park area are formed within loosely bound Quarternary sands that have collected in the basin between ranges.

The water that gathers in the hollows (*huecos*) of the rocky surfaces in the park is an integral part of a distinctive microenvironment within the context of the Chihuahuan Desert, one of the great deserts of North America. Rainfall in this portion of the Chihuahuan Desert is slight, and its timing ensures that effective moisture will be even lower than annual totals might indicate. Most of the precipitation occurs in the summer, when evaporation rates are highest. In addition, half the year's rain may fall during a single, brief thunderstorm. Flash flooding is characteristic, as much of the water rapidly drains away and little soaks in.

Plants. Although the forms of vegetation are typical of the modern Chihuahuan Desert, the modern ecology is quite different from that of the not too distant past. Until the surrounding flats were overgrazed, the area had the characteristics of an arid grassland rather than the dry (xeric), desert conditions presently so apparent. Today, dominated by the creosote bush (*Larrea tridentata*), the area surrounding the park is an excellent example of a xeric plant community. Stunted mesquite (*Prosopis* *glandulosa*), tarbush (*Flourensia cernua*), and an occasional soaptree yucca (*Yucca elata*) are the other most prominent woody plants. Stunted, relict oak (*Quercus* spp.) and juniper (*Juniperus* spp.) can be found in protected areas. Grasses include gypsum grama (*Bouteloua breviseta*), burro grass (*Scleropogon brevifolius*), and fluffgrass (*Erioneuron pulchellum*).

Animals. Excavations at Hueco Tanks have indicated that peoples in the past used many of the same species found in the area today, including pronghorn antelope (*Antilocapra americana*), deer (*Odocoileus* spp.), diamondback rattlesnake (*Crotalus atrox*), jackrabbit (*Lepus californicus*), mountain lion (*Felis concolor*), raccoon (*Procyon lotor*), and black bear (*Ursus americanus*).

Archeology: Hueco Tanks is known as site 41EP2 in the trinomial site-numbering system adopted in most of the United States almost four decades ago. In this system the first number (41) represents the alphabetical order of the state in which the site is located. The next designation (EP) indicates the county (El Paso) within the state, and the last number is the serial order in which the site was recorded. Thus the designation 41EP2 translates as the second site recorded in this system in El Paso County, Texas.

But is 41EP2 a site or a locality with a number of sites? In this sense it is a good example of a problem explored in Chapter 5 of this book. What is an archeological site? Here at Hueco Tanks there are a number of discrete areas that, had they been found in a modern survey of archeological sites, would have merited a separate site designation for each. Since Hueco Tanks represents such a distinctive environment, perhaps it makes sense to consider it as a single site rather than as a number of sites, as often happens at other similarly confused localities. At any rate, it is important to remember that archeologists are using an arbitrary designation when they call a given place an archeological site. When artifacts are found at such a place, they cannot be assumed to be related in a cultural or even a temporal sense. Associations must be established to support inferences drawn from similarities with other, better-known cultures.

For example, a summary of the discoveries here at Hueco Tanks certainly suggests some similarity with Puebloan cultures in New Mexico, and that similarity has led to the classification of the occupation here in the Doña Ana Phase of the Jornada Branch of the Mogollon Culture. The Doña Ana Phase has been poorly defined as a transitional period. Not much is known about it in an unmixed context. From that perspective, the isolation of Hueco Tanks is an archeologist's dream come true. It may represent a single-component site; that is, the occupation of the site may be traced to a single group of people who lived here for a specific period.

Archeologists use terms such as Doña Ana Phase to refer to assemblages of artifacts that seem to them to represent a single people. Here at Hueco Tanks the Doña Ana people were quite likely responsible for most of the rock painting that makes the site so interesting to most visitors today. Perhaps even more important, from an archeologist's point of view, is the opportunity to excavate a single-component site. The following summary is derived from such excavations at Hueco Tanks.

Hueco Tanks village was established by agricultural people and continuously occupied by them from about A.D. 1150 to about A.D. 1350. Thus, for approximately 200 years the people at Hueco Tanks lived a simple farming village existence. The village was small but remarkably self-sufficient. The occupation seems to have been concentrated in the northeast part of the present park at the north end of the easternmost rock formation, as shown in Figure 31. Here the people were able to cultivate their crops in the rich alluvial wash from the hills to the east. The fields were in the places where even today the plants are noticeably greener and of a different type than in the surrounding soils. Not only is the soil, the Mimbres soil, richer than the other soils in the area but also runoff water from the hills backed up against the granite and supplied additional, much-needed moisture to ensure the yearly harvest.

In addition to their clever utilization of available moisture for crops and of water naturally collected in the *huecos* for drinking, the villagers constructed sophisticated cisterns and drainage systems to fill them. Nooks and crannies of the rock outcroppings were dammed, and the natural courses of runoff were diverted so that the water flowed into the artificial basins. Painted figures often are found near those and other water reservoirs.

Typical structures at Hueco Tanks village were single-roomed, rectangular pit houses with up to 25 square meters of floor space (Fig. 32). They had adobe walls and floors with crèches set into the walls and with storage pits and fireplaces built into the floor. Roofs of unknown construction were supported by two posts aligned along an axis near the room centerline. The entrance seems to have been on the south side of the houses.

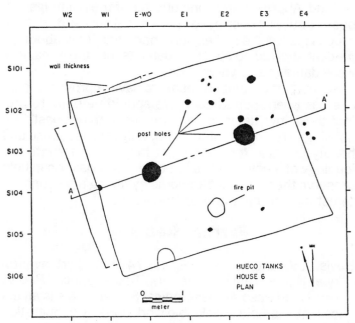

32. House 6, Hueco Tanks. (Courtesy Texas Parks and Wildlife.)

Rock Art at Hueco Tanks

The rock art at this locale is quite satisfying and the most interesting feature of the park. The questions of origin and meaning of the paintings perhaps can never be answered; they are as obscure as the paintings at other prehistoric and protohistoric sites, such as Seminole Canyon (described in the Edwards Plateau/Hill Country section). Prevailing interpretation relates the paintings to similar motifs in the Mimbres area of New Mexico and to the historically known Kachinas of various pueblos. (Although this apparent relationship may be valid in a general sense, an association between the Hueco Tanks villagers and a particular Puebloan group has not been firmly established.)

Several years ago, amateurs in the El Paso area conducted an inventory of rock art at Hueco Tanks. They concluded that of approximately 1,200 figures reported up to that time, only about 75 percent of the paintings remained. Approximately one quarter of the paintings had been entirely destroyed by vandalism and natural processes. Of the still existing paintings, only about 50 percent showed no apparent damage, but the remainder were damaged to varying degrees.

Although the situation seems to have improved as park use has been monitored, more should be done to protect these invaluable remembrances of things past. The paintings are important to us not only for their grace and beauty but also for the insight they can offer into the ideology of a now vanished people. Each visitor can help preserve these ancient artworks by taking a personal interest in their care and preservation.

Further Reading

Davis, J. V., and K. S. Toness. 1974. A rock art inventory at Hueco Tanks State Park, Texas. Special Report No. 12, El Paso Archaeological Society. This is an excellent example of valuable work done by cooperation between amateurs and professionals. In this case amateurs reinventoried and evaluated the condition of the rock art at Hueco Tanks, making a valuable contribution to our understanding of the changes in the site in the recent past.

Kegley, G. 1982. *Archeological Investigations at 41EP2 Hueco Tanks State Historical Park, El Paso County, Texas.* Austin: Texas Parks and Wildlife Department. This report on recent excavations at a small village complex at Hueco Tanks is interesting, but the investigation was too truncated.

Miller, G. O. 1985. Hueco Tanks serves up art on the rocks. *Texas Highways* 32(8):18–27. This is a well-illustrated, popular account of the state park. Well done, recommended.

Newcomb, W. W. 1967. *The Rock Art of Texas Indians.* Austin: University of Texas Press. This book is the classic volume dealing with Native American rock art in Texas. Hueco Tanks material is well represented, as is material from sites throughout the state. Highly recommended.

Appendices

Museums

Well over 500 institutions in Texas are maintained for public use as museums (Tyler and Tyler 1983). Although many include exhibits of archeological materials from Texas and may offer an opportunity to see a special or unusual type of artifact, only a few of the larger museums offer a broad range of services that include lectures, publications, and original research programs in addition to curation and display of Texas archeological materials. Only those larger museums are included here. In addition, the reader is encouraged to visit the usually excellent interpretive centers featured at most of the sites described in this book.

PANHANDLE-PLAINS REGION

Panhandle-Plains Historical
  Museum
2401 Fourth Avenue
Canyon, Texas 79016
(806) 656-2244

This, the oldest state-supported museum in Texas, is on the campus of West Texas State University. The museum and the university have each sponsored regional archeological research and publications since the founding of the museum in 1919, and the depth and variety of exhibits reflect the ensuing decades of thoughtful acquisition and careful research.

This museum is remarkably sophisticated, but located as it is in one of the least-populated, more-desolate areas of Texas, it is often overlooked. That is unfortunate, for it is one of the fine regional museums in Texas and features a broad array of exhibit halls, including Pioneer Village, Hall of Pre-History, Hall of Ethnology and Archeology, Hall of Fine Arts, Hall of the Founders, and Hall of Texas State Government.

The natural history of the Southern Plains is well represented in excellent displays of modern flora and fauna. In addition, there are exceptional dioramas and articulated fossil skeletons of Pleistocene megafauna characteristic of the Panhandle-Plains at the time of Paleoindian occupations such as the Clovis and Folsom complexes.

For those interested in history and historical archeology, the Pioneer Village presents nineteenth-century artifacts in their functional context. Original cabins, moved from their original sites, have been resited in the museum with attention to authenticity. Hotels, barbershops, professional offices of doctors and lawyers, stores, and a post office have been recreated with original artifacts. The wealth of detail contained in the artifacts cannot be captured in photographs or written descriptions, and this display is invaluable in interpretation of late-eighteenth-century historic material found in archeological sites. The tools displayed in the blacksmith shop alone offer important insight into the function and manufacture of the metal tools so often found in historic sites.

The ethnographic displays feature Plains Indian artifacts representing Comanche, Kiowa, and other tribes living in the area at the time of earliest historic contact. Pipes, blankets, pottery, and ritual objects may be studied. Archeological materials in this display include Paleoindian artifacts as well as an excellent variety of Archaic and Late Prehistoric stone tools from sites in the region. Many of the latter artifacts may be observed in the basement in informal groupings that represent separate site collections.

The museum store features regional items such as fossil kits, maps, modern Puebloan pottery, and other modern Native American artifacts. Included in the wide range of books available are a number of titles of concern to archeology in general as well as to regional archeology. Well-crafted, plastic replicas of Paleoindian points such as *Clovis, Folsom,* and *Plainview,* each with accompanying explanation, are also for sale.

The museum is open daily from 9 A.M. to 5 P.M., except Sundays, when the hours are 2 to 6 P.M. Closed New Year's Day, Christmas, and Thanksgiving Day. Free, but contributions accepted. Membership in Panhandle-Plains Historical Society may be obtained for an annual fee of $5. Members receive a subscription to the *Panhandle-Plains Historical Review* and information concerning museum events.

The Museum
Texas Tech University
Fourth Street at Indiana
  Avenue
Lubbock, Texas 79409
(806) 742-2442

As one of the fastest-growing museums in Texas, this place offers many exciting features not usually associated with university museums. Most notable is its proximity to the Lubbock Lake Site, one of the most important Paleoindian sites in North America. Personnel associated with Texas Tech University and The Museum have been the principal investigators at Lubbock Lake through the years of its exploration and have been an influence in the development of the museum.

The interpretive displays on the current and past environments of the Llano Estacado are especially pertinent to archeologists interested in the paleoecology of the region. *Clovis* points from the Clovis Site are displayed, as are articulated Pleistocene fossils. Mammoth, bison, and horse displays are especially effective. A section of the Clovis Site clearly shows the association between the mammoth and the *Clovis* projectile point type.

An innovative feature of interest to historical archeologists is the outdoor display of more than twenty early historic structures and authentic associated artifacts in the Ranching Heritage Center. Approximately thirty historic buildings, ranging from basic one-room structures to elaborate multistory houses, have been moved from their original site and restored here on twelve landscaped acres. Of special interest is a wide collection of mounted windmills.

The museum is open from 8:30 A.M. to 4:30 P.M. Monday through Friday and 1 to 4:30 P.M. Saturday and Sunday. The museum is free, but there is a small fee for admission to the Ranching Heritage Center.

CENTRAL PRAIRIES REGION

Heard Natural Science
  Museum and Wildlife
  Sanctuary
Farm Road 1378
McKinney, Texas 75069
(214) 542-5012

Although this small private museum does not have significant displays of archeological material, it does boast an accessible opportunity to study the past and present environment of the Central Prairies. There are excellent exhibits of regional geology and biology and more than two miles of nature trails. Except on Sunday afternoon, nature trails are open only by reservation; visitors must be accompanied by a guide at all times.

Open Tuesday through Saturday from 9 A.M. to 5 P.M. and Sunday from 1 to 5 P.M. Closed New Year's Day, Easter, Fourth of July, Thanksgiving Day, Christmas Eve, and Christmas Day. Free.

PINEYWOODS REGION

Williamson Museum
Department of History and
  Social Science

Northwestern State
  University
Natchitoches, Louisiana
  71469
(318) 357-4364

Although the status of the park at the historic site of
Los Adaes remains uncertain, this museum has permanent displays of materials recovered there in the course
of excavations sponsored by the university. The anthropology, archeology, and history of other sites in the
region of northwestern Louisiana are well represented
in numerous displays.

In addition to the museum itself, a visit to Natchitoches
(NAK-ah-tish) is in many ways like a visit back in time. Information concerning many antebellum structures in the
vicinity is available at the museum.

The Williamson Museum is generally open from 9 A.M.
to 5 P.M. when the university is in session. Free.

EDWARDS PLATEAU/HILL COUNTRY

Strecker Museum
Richardson Science
  Building
S. Fourth at Spade
Baylor University
Waco, Texas 76798
(817) 755-1110

This relatively unknown museum has excellent displays
of archeological materials from Central Texas in addition
to extensive collections of prehistoric artifacts from Central Texas sites. Extensive natural history displays and
collections are featured in this, one of the oldest museums in the state. Recent programs include the beginning
of an outdoor display of early, regional historic structures,
similar in concept to the Ranching Heritage Center at

Texas Tech Museum and the outdoor replicas at the Institute of Texan Cultures.

The museum is open from 9 A.M. to 4 P.M. Monday
through Friday, 10 A.M. to 1 P.M. Saturday, 2 to 5 P.M. Sunday. Holiday schedule is erratic; call for information. Free.

Texas Memorial Museum
2400 Trinity
Austin, Texas 78705
(512) 471-1604

Administratively linked with the University of Texas, this
is one of the outstanding museums in the state. It has
sponsored some of the most exciting archeological work
in the region, and many of the artifacts from those excavations are on view. It is an active research and pub-
lishing agency, but its activity is inconsistent, waxing and
waning according to Texas' political whims.

The entire museum is full of unexpected delights. The
fourth floor is devoted to the anthropology of Texas.
Although in need of updating, the exhibits not only portray the interpretation of archeological materials but also
display the original artifacts. Some dioramas recreate the
habitation of sites such as the Fate Bell Shelter in Val
Verde County, and others reenact such action sequences
as a buffalo drive over the rim and into the canyon at
Bonfire Shelter, also in Val Verde County. Anthropological materials from various Indian tribes of Texas also are
featured in a section on this floor.

The third floor is devoted to the flora and fauna of the
state. There are comprehensive displays of various
animals and plants, some set in attractive full-scale dioramas. The section is especially useful for conceptualiz-
ing archeological materials in their environmental
context.

The first floor features geology and paleontology. Especially useful are the maps showing the distribution of
various rocks in the state. Articulated Pleistocene skeletons are useful in understanding the paleoecology of
Texas.

The museum store is small but features a wide selection of books for sale with many otherwise hard-to-find titles in archeology and anthropology. Bookstores in the university area are among the best sources in Texas for literature dealing with various aspects of archeology and anthropology.

If archeology were the only reason to visit a museum, and you could visit only one museum in Texas, this one would be the one to visit. Open Monday through Friday from 9 A.M. to 5 P.M., 1 to 5 P.M. Saturday and Sunday. Closed most major holidays. Adults $1 admission, students 50 cents.

Witte Museum
3801 Broadway
San Antonio, Texas 78209
(512) 226-5544

This delightful museum is the center for history, natural science, anthropology, and archeology of the three museums of the San Antonio Museum Association. Long active in research in South Texas archeology, the Witte is currently mounting a major display of Pecos River cultures in conjunction with the museum-sponsored publication of *Ancient Texans: Rock Art and Lifeways Along the Lower Pecos* (Shafer 1986), an excellent, well-illustrated, and comprehensive volume of that culture area. The Lower Pecos exhibit is arguably the best archeological exhibit in the state.

In addition to research into the prehistoric archeology of South Texas, the Witte has sponsored work in historic archeology. Particular emphasis has focused on the Spanish colonial period in San Antonio, and the Witte is a center of exhibits from that period. Particularly interesting is a display of visual representations of the Alamo. Its outstanding feature is a museum-sponsored, controversial painting of the final siege in which historical probability is accorded more importance than heroic myth.

The excellent museum shop offers a wide variety of publications in anthropology, archeology, and various environmental aspects of South Texas. The Witte's schedule varies, but it is generally open daily, except Monday, from 10 A.M. to 5 P.M. The museum is closed New Year's Day, Battle of Flowers Day, Independence Day, Labor Day, Thanksgiving Day, and Christmas Day. Admission: adults $3, special adults $1.50, children (6–12) $1, toddlers and infants free. Free admission for everyone on Thursdays from 3 to 9 P.M.

The University of Texas
  Institute of Texan Cultures
Hemisfair Plaza
801 S. Bowie Street
San Antonio, Texas 78205
(512) 226-7651

Patterned in concept after the magnificent Museum of Anthropology in Mexico City but falling far short of the excitement of that national treasure, this museum represents the Texas legacy of Hemisfair 1968. Although the history of some of Texas' various ethnic groups is the featured attraction (the museum is therefore of major interest to students of historical archeology), there is also an interesting section on prehistory. Appropriately enough, it is presented as the first of Texas' cultures. Examples of the various periods are presented in standard interpretive form, and original artifacts from throughout the state are shown.

Outside special exhibits with imaginative replicas have been constructed to capture the flavor of a frontier fort and a schoolhouse.

The institute is open daily, except Monday, from 9 A.M. to 5 P.M. Free.

SOUTH TEXAS REGION

Brazosport Museum of
  Natural Science
400 College Drive
Clute, Texas 77566
(409) 265-7831

This small regional museum, a part of the Brazosport Center for the Arts and Sciences, offers an excellent opportunity to view various aspects of the ecology of the Texas coast. An extensive exhibit from the nearby Dow-Cleaver Site provides those interested in the prehistory of Texas' central Gulf coast an unusual opportunity to study artifacts in their area of origin.

The museum is open Tuesday through Saturday from 10 A.M. to 5 P.M., Sunday from 2 to 5 P.M. Free.

Corpus Christi Museum
1900 N. Chaparral
Corpus Christi, Texas
  78401
(512) 883-2862

This rapidly growing regional museum has won national awards for its exhibits in natural sciences, anthropology, and archeology. It is unsurpassed in its presentation of the habitat of the Texas Gulf coast, including present and past environments and cultures. Most spectacular, perhaps, is the attractive display of artifacts associated with the famous sixteenth-century Spanish shipwrecks off nearby Padre Island.

The museum is open Tuesday through Saturday from 10 A.M. to 5 P.M. and Sunday from 2 to 5 P.M. Free.

TRANS-PECOS REGION

Museum of the Big Bend
Sul Ross State University
Alpine, Texas 79832
(915) 837-8143

This regional museum has seen better times. During the thirties Sul Ross was the center of some of the most active archeological work in the state. Although much of the work was far below today's standards, personnel from Sul Ross and the Alpine community carried out some of the most extensive excavations ever in the region. Unfortunately, most artifacts curated here are inaccessible today. Nevertheless, this neglected little museum remains one of the best in the Trans-Pecos.

Besides extensive natural history exhibits, featuring the ecology of the Chihuahuan Desert, there are exhibits of the history and prehistory of the Big Bend, highlighting periods of early settlement and the Mexican Revolution as revealed through artifacts and photographs.

The Chihuahuan Desert Museum Laboratory, an undertaking of the independently organized Chihuahuan Desert Research Institute, studies the distinctive plants of the Chihuahuan Desert in a controlled, native environment. Information about this facility, near Fort Davis, is available at the museum or from the director of the institute at 837-8370.

Open Tuesday through Saturday 9 A.M. to 5 P.M., Sunday 1 to 5 P.M. Free, donations accepted.

El Paso Centennial Museum
University and Wiggins
    Avenue
El Paso, Texas 79968
(915) 747-5565

One of those museums founded as part of the observance of the Texas Centennial, this museum is now affiliated with the University of Texas at El Paso. A distinctly regional museum, its exhibits feature the natural history of the El Paso area. Impressive displays of artifacts represent Southwestern Indian cultures, the Spanish colonial period, and early nineteenth-century Anglo settlements.

Open when the university is in session, Tuesday through Friday 10 A.M. to 5:30 P.M. and Sunday 1:30 to 5:30 P.M. Free.

Further Reading

The following books were useful in providing information for this section. They are recommended for further information about these and other museums in Texas.

Shafer, H. J. 1986. *Ancient Texans: Rock Art and Lifeways Along the Lower Pecos.* San Antonio: Witte Museum. This volume presents an up-to-date account of the Archaic cultures of Seminole Canyon. Many of the types of artifacts displayed at the Witte Museum are illustrated and explained here. Highly recommended.
Sharpe, Patricia, and Robert S. Weddle. 1982. *Texas: The Newest, the Biggest, the Most Complete Guide to All of Texas.* Austin: Texas Monthly Press. As the title asserts, this is a good general guide to Texas. Not only are various regional museums briefly described but other diversions are also included. Recommended.
Texas Department of Highways and Public Transportation. 1986. *Texas Travel Handbook.* Austin: Travel and Information Division, Texas Department of Highways and Public Transportation. This free publication is the most up-to-date general guide for travel in Texas. It is published and distributed by the Highway Department and is concise and purely descriptive—just the facts, ma'am. Texas towns are listed alphabetically; many local museums are mentioned.
Tyler, P. E., and R. Tyler. 1983. *Texas Museums: A Guide-*

book. Austin: University of Texas Press. Already somewhat out of date, this little book remains the best guide
to the vast number of Texas museums. Many small,
local museums as well as the large, well-known ones
are listed and described here. A must for the inveter-
ate museumgoer.

Academic Programs in Archeology and Anthropology

Almost all academic programs in archeology in Texas are affiliated with anthropology. Anthropology is the umbrella discipline; archeology is couched in its terms, and it is often necessary to inquire within an anthropology department to get information about archeology.

Many Texas colleges and universities offer introductory courses in anthropology. Only a few have programs in anthropology and archeology, and they are listed below, in alphabetical order by city.

Arlington
Department of Sociology and Anthropology
University of Texas–Arlington
Box 19088-UTA Station
Arlington, Texas 76019
(817) 273-2118

Austin
Department of Anthropology
University of Texas at Austin
Austin, Texas 78712-1086
(512) 471-4206

Canyon
Department of Geosciences
West Texas State University
WT Station
Canyon, Texas 79016
(806) 656-0111

College Station
Department of Anthropology
Texas A&M University
College Station, Texas 77843
(409) 845-1031

Commerce
    Department of Sociology and Anthropology
    East Texas State University
    East Texas Station
    Commerce, Texas 75428
    (214) 886-5081

Dallas
    Social Science Division
    Richland College
    12800 Abrams Road
    Dallas, Texas 75243
    (214) 238-6290

    Department of Anthropology
    Southern Methodist University
    Box 296
    Dallas, Texas 75275
    (214) 692-2058

Denton
    Department of Geography and Anthropology
    University of North Texas
    Box 13797-NT Station
    Denton, Texas 76203
    (817) 565-2681

El Paso
    Department of Sociology and Anthropology
    University of Texas–El Paso
    El Paso, Texas 79968
    (915) 747-5576

Houston
    Department of Anthropology
    Rice University
    Box 1892
    Houston, Texas 77251
    (713) 527-8101

Department of Anthropology
University of Houston
4800 Calhoun
Houston, Texas 77004
(713) 749-2321

Lubbock
Department of Anthropology
Texas Tech University
Box 4350
Lubbock, Texas 79409
(806) 742-3661

Nacogdoches
Department of Sociology
Stephen F. Austin State University
Box 13047-SFA Station
Nacogdoches, Texas 75962
(409) 568-2504

Natchitoches
Department of History and Social Sciences
Northwestern State University
Natchitoches, Louisiana 71497
(318) 357-4364

San Antonio
Center for Archeological Research
Division of Behavioral and Cultural Sciences
University of Texas–San Antonio
San Antonio, Texas 78285
(512) 691-4375

San Marcos
Department of Sociology and Anthropology
Southwest Texas State University
San Marcos, Texas 78666
(512) 245-2364

Waco
Department of Sociology, Anthropology,
Social Work, and Gerontology
Baylor University
Box 6367
Waco, Texas 76706
(817) 755-1811

Archeological Societies

The following list contains the names and addresses of some of the more active archeological organizations in Texas. Most have programs open to the general public and information about other, related organizations. Of those societies listed, the Texas Archeological Society and the Southern Texas Archaeological Association are the largest and most active. They sponsor field schools, hold regular meetings, and publish journals.

Central Texas Archeological Society
4229 Mitchell Road
Waco, Texas 76710

Coastal Bend Archeological Society
3413 Cartagena
Corpus Christi, Texas 78418

Concho Valley Archeological Society
326 Troy Street
San Angelo, Texas 76901

Dallas Archeological Society
Box 28026
Dallas, Texas 75228

El Paso Archeological Society
Box 4345
El Paso, Texas 79914

Houston Archeological Society
Box 6751
Houston, Texas 77265

Iraan Archaeological Society
Box 183
Iraan, Texas 79744

Midland Archeological Society
Box 4224
Midland, Texas 79704

Panhandle Archeological Society
Box 814
Amarillo, Texas 79105

Richland Anthropological Society
Richland College
12800 Abrams Road
Dallas, Texas 75243

Southern Texas Archaeological Association
123 E. Crestline
San Antonio, Texas 78201

Tarrant County Archeological Society
413 E. Lavender
Arlington, Texas 76010

Texas Archeological Society
Center for Archeological Research
University of Texas at San Antonio
San Antonio, Texas 78285

Travis County Archeological Society
TARL
10100 Burnet Road
Austin, Texas 78758-4497

History of the San Antonio Missions

Date	Event
May 1, 1718	Father Antonio Olivares establishes Mission San Antonio de Valero, the Alamo (earlier known as Mission San Francisco Solano when it was located at the present-day village of Guerrero, Coahuila, Mexico).
May 5, 1718	The Presidio and Villa de Bexar (modern San Antonio) is established by Martin de Alarcón, governor of Texas and Coahuila.
1720	Mission San José is established a few miles downstream from the Alamo.
1724	Alamo is moved to its present site.
March 9, 1731	Fifteen families from the Canary Islands arrive in San Antonio.
1731	Missions Concepción, San Juan, and Espada are established.
1731–1745	Extensive irrigation systems (*acequias*) are constructed. (The Espada dam and aqueduct are completed during this period.)
1768	Construction begins on present church structure at San José.
May 27, 1793	Mission San Antonio de Valero (the Alamo) is secularized, its lands are divided.
August 24, 1821	Mexico wins independence from Spain.
1824	Other missions are secularized, most abandoned.
March 6, 1836	Final siege of the Alamo.
1858	Father Francis Bouchu, assigned to San Fernando church, begins restoration of Mission Espada and holds services there.
1887	Church at Mission Concepción is partially restored and rededicated.
1913	Church at Mission Concepción is further restored and put into regular, active use.
1937	After reconstruction and stabilization, church at San José reopens for services.
1978	All missions except Alamo come under administration of National Park Service.

Index